Table

Introduction

Thank you

Thanks to Matt and Steve Yoannou for their work on the cover design of this book and all the other images inside it. Thanks to Travis Cranmer and Danish Ghazi for the encouragement along the way. Thanks to Maxie Bai for her editing proficiency, and to everyone else who made this book possible.

Zack,

All the best on your path to FI!

Graeme Falco

Dear readers,

I am not infallible by any means. However, the majority of my beliefs and analyses are backed by academic research, corroborated through the scientific method. If you have any counterpoints or points of discussion that are based on empirical evidence, I would love to hear it. Please contact me at graemecpa@gmail.com.

Follow me on twitter @graemeCPA, and reddit /u/graemeCPA. You can also join my mailing list[1] or visit www.graemefalco.com.

Disclaimer

Although my chartered professional accountancy has given me analytical tools and persuasive writing skills, I am not a financial advisor. I am also not a tax expert. This is especially true concerning US tax matters, which are significantly more complicated than those in Canada. It's not simply a legal matter but also a philosophical one. I believe everyone should ultimately make their own educated financial choices and not simply defer to the perceived wisdom of others. Your confidence will make you a better and happier investor.

This publication is designed to provide accurate and authoritative information in regard to the subject matter covered. It is sold with the understanding that neither the author nor the publisher is engaged in rendering legal, accounting, or other professional service. If legal advice or other expert assistance is required, the services of a competent professional person should be sought.

---

[1] http://eepurl.com/coq6lL

It all started with a joke

Our high school math teacher stood at the front of the class with a grin on his face as he tried to gain the attention of 30 students giddy from gym class.

Hey class, a salesman gets up to take a smoke break and an eager accountant quickly asks him if he realizes how much money that is costing him.

Salesman: "Yes I do, as a matter of fact. $12 a pack."

Accountant: "How many packs a day?"

Salesman: "One and a half."

Accountant: "And how many years have you been smoking?"

Salesman: "Fifteen good ones!"

Accountant: "So one-and-a-half packs a day at $12 a pack puts your spending per month at $540. Or approximately $6,500 a year, correct?"

Salesman: "Yeah, if you say so."

Accountant: "So over the past 15 years, you've spent $97,500, not accounting for inflation, correct?"

Salesman: "Right," he said nervously.

Accountant: "And if you had invested that money monthly, earning 6% interest, you would now have $155,500. You could've bought a Ferrari. But now all that money is up in smoke!"

Salesman: "Crap, you're right!"

The salesman scratched his head and pondered for a moment before asking: "Do you smoke?"

Accountant: "No."

Salesman: "Oh–then where's your Ferrari?!"

The salesman walked passed the slack-jawed accountant and enjoyed his cigarette.

The room of kids groaned and then laughed. But instead of laughing I was at the back of the class, desperately wondering where the Ferrari had gone.

State of the union: Who can benefit from this book?

You've seen the headlines. It's no secret that the middle class in North America is shrinking. Wealth disparity is accelerating as the top 1% of wealthiest Americans have come to own over 40% of American assets. The average American student graduates with $35,000 in debt and many owe hundreds of thousands of dollars before ever seeing their first paycheck. When today's historically high consumer debt is added on top, the future of the middle class starts to look bleak.

The reality is that nearly half of Americans have to borrow money to cover an unexpected expense of $400, and the statistics in Canada aren't much prettier.

The good news is that although the top 1% owns a disproportionately unfair share of wealth, you don't need to be a part of that group in order to have a meaningful, joyful, and content life. Let's be very clear about this: at any moment, there is a segment of the populace waiting in the rain to catch a bus to their third part-time job of the day for the privilege of making $6 per hour. And they aren't reading this book on the bus because an e-reader is the difference between whether or not their kid gets to eat.

The advice in this book does nothing to address the structural barriers that maintain poverty in both Canada and America. In 2015, the poverty line was $11,700 for a single person in the United States and there is simply no amount of financial planning, investing, or lifestyle changes that can do anything more than slap a Band-Aid on the problems experienced by our most needy.

Although the main principles of financial independence can be useful for anyone, the middle class benefits tremendously from this mindset. And people in the upper-middle class, making astonishingly large salaries like $45,000 a year, can benefit even more. To put this in context, in 2015, Americans earning $45,000 earned more than nearly 70% of their fellow workers! This is the type of earning power that can make dreams come true.

What's wrong? Did I lose you? If you are sitting there scoffing and asking yourself—*What dreams could possibly come true on a 45K salary? Not the American dream, that's for damn sure*—then you need to keep reading.

Even more outrageously, this advice is for the people in this country who have incomes in the 85th percentile, earning over $75,000 a year in the US, and want to make the most of their incredible earning power. If you are one of these rich fat cats and you find yourself wondering where that Ferrari went because your credit card is blowing up and you can't imagine how people earning 10% less than you even get by on such meager earnings, then you're reading the right book.

How to use this guide

As you may have gleaned from the Table of Contents, this book will cover everything from the relationship between money and happiness, whether you should buy or rent a place to live, and how the future of robotic automation may impact your job prospects. This guide is structured to give you an introductory but thorough understanding of the 'what, why, and how' for everything to do with financial independence (FI). Before we get started, we have a bit of housecleaning to do:

1. Rather than compile a list of definitions into a glossary for you, I've merely italicized the common financial terms. Look up any italicized phrase on your phone or computer if you're curious or want some more context. There won't be any excessively academic words or phrases, I promise!

2. The appendices include more detailed information on topics discussed in the body of this book, such as the merits of socially responsible investing. It doesn't matter whether you read the book chronologically or skip to an appendix after reading a reference to it in the body of the book.

Chapter 1

Financial Independence: What is it and why do I want it?

Most people list money as the single greatest source of stress in their lives. Yet, many have no desire to learn more about the underlying source of that stress and how to minimize it. Even more people are overwhelmed by contradictory advertisements and the non-stop barrage of sensationalist news stories. Everywhere you look there is someone telling you about hot stock tips or secrets on how to make money online. It's no surprise that the same people who are stressed out about money are also found muttering: "Investing? Saving? Ugh. Numbers are for nerds and old people. I can't be bothered."

Financial independence (FI), involves doing research, learning about yourself, and doing some (not too onerous) work to determine the relationship that you want to have with money. It requires investigating the sources of happiness in your life and setting priorities that allow you to maximize the happiness you'll receive from them. It means both understanding the psychological impact of modern consumerism culture and calculating how much money you need to stop working. And yes, there will be some numbers along the way, but don't worry. It'll be worth it.

Despite growing economic inequality, citizens of any western country in the 21st century are the wealthiest and most fortunate humans to ever have existed.

Technology and real wage growth advances allow us to live lives that weren't even imagined one hundred years ago. Surely, if our great-grandparents knew the kind of lives we would live now, with a laundry machine in every home and 8-hour work-days, they never would have guessed that we would be so worried about money. So why do most of us feel like we'll never have enough?

FI means having enough. More specifically, FI is achieved when income earned from passive sources exceeds one's expenses. Passive income comes from anything that doesn't require a lot of time or effort, such as real estate, stocks, bonds, or a business that mostly runs itself. Simply put, you have reached FI once you have a sum of money that is large enough to work for you (by bringing in income) so that you are no longer reliant on *your* work to make ends meet.

For some people, being FI may coincide with retirement, but that's not a requirement. Having your expenses covered means that money is no longer a source of stress in your life. But you don't have to achieve FI to obtain these psychological benefits. Even making progress towards your financial security, and eventually your full financial independence, can allow you to untangle the strong emotional and psychological association between money and happiness and brings you closer to self-actualization.

Here we turn back to our high school psych class and Abraham Maslow, an American psychologist, who is best known for his theory on human health and need. Now, what does this guy have to do with FI? As a psychologist, Maslow created the pyramid in Figure 1 to rank his hierarchy of innate human needs. To state it plainly, we want to attain FI to achieve self-actualization.

Figure 1: Maslow's hierarchy of needs.

Maslow's hierarchy of needs represents challenges faced by millions of real people every day. For many North Americans, their desperate financial situation is a threat to their safety, and worse, more basic physiological needs like sleep and food. By starting on the path to FI, you are consciously helping yourself move up Maslow's hierarchy and learning to prioritize your health, self-expression through art, for example, or sports; you are focusing on your relationships and becoming more aware of your social, emotional, and mental needs; these are also all things that fall by the wayside when you're constantly worrying about your next paycheck. Life is too short to worry about money.

In human history, most people on this rock we call Earth have never been afforded the opportunity to rise above a level or two on Maslow's hierarchy. Attaining FI gives you those options; with FI, you can volunteer, travel, or stay in the job that you currently have and enjoy—or not. Maybe your passion is eating Cheetos and playing video games. You can do that with FI. Not having to worry about money will let you focus on what is important to you. This gives you the potential for self-actualization, which can be broadly defined as reaching your full potential as a human being. That's an admittedly vague concept, and for most people probably includes numerous sets of values and behaviours instead of one specific goal or calling. Use your imagination and try to think of a few of the things you would do if you were being the best version of yourself. Achieving FI will hopefully allow you to do those things more often.

If you've read thus far, I hope we can agree that FI is a worthy goal that can be pursued by most of us. The two big questions everyone should be thinking now are: "Where do I start?" And, "how do I know when I've reached FI?"

How do you get to FI? Well, everyone's got their own ideas. We all know people who swear by real estate or proclaim that "the only way to make it big is to start your own business!" It can be a daunting thing to even think about. Investments can seem like mysterious black boxes and financial advisors appear to purposefully explain things in the most complicated way possible.

Figure 2: The wide-eyed look seen in financial advisors' offices across the country.

The truth is that FI is not an art. It's a science. There is empirical, peer-reviewed evidence available to answer almost every question you have about money, psychology, and the relationship between the two. Ignore the newspapers and the advisors getting rich off of your hard work. Let's stop guessing and get it right. Let's apply the scientific method to your money so we can properly answer both of these questions.

Early retirement? That sounds like a pipe dream!

The concepts of retirement and financial independence (FI) are intertwined because in order to have a stable and stress-free retirement, you will need to be FI. A consequence of becoming FI is that retirement becomes a decision, whether it is early or not at all. Are you thinking, "Wait a minute, early retirement is fantasy!"? Don't worry, that's a rational initial reaction. Truth be told, even retiring at the now traditional 65 years of age *was* a far off fantasy just a few generations ago.

Historically, the 8-hour work day is rooted in the industrial revolution of mid-19th century Britain as early unions advocated for the emancipation of the working class from dangerous factory conditions and long hours. Although almost two hundred years have passed, the developed world continues to use the simple model of splitting the 24-hour day into thirds: 8 hours for rest, 8 hours for recreation, and 8 hours for labour.

Due to technological advancement and associated efficiencies, the smog clouds over London have cleared. The economies of Western nations have shifted towards service-oriented jobs and worker productivity has skyrocketed exponentially in the last 150 years. But the '9 to 5' routine—the legacy of the first unions—is still ingrained in our society.

As technology continues to advance and more of our work is performed by software, people will eventually question what constitutes a full work day. It will take time for this to change and some cultures may never embrace a variation from the status quo, but countries like Sweden have led the way by experimenting with a 6-hour work day. Interestingly, they report no decrease in productivity and find instead that people get their work done faster and waste less time.

Work is not an evil concept, or even a bad one. Most people enjoy some aspect of their work and gain a sense of self-esteem and respect from their workplace accomplishments and relationships. However, for each person who loves their job, there are those who would gladly give up the daily grind of waking up in the dark, racing through a gridlock of sleep-deprived zombies, and clicking away on spreadsheets under fluorescent lights.

Figure 3: Braaaiiinsss.

If you think that sounds like a pessimistic or worst-case view on the modern working world, you may be blissfully unaware of the extreme cynicism engaged in by the conspiracy theorists among us. There are people who believe that the 8-hour work day is designed to keep the masses consuming and shareholders' profits high. They believe corporate America has designed our lifestyles to make us perfect consumers: dissatisfied but hopeful, earning a fair amount but indulging in spending during their free time, disoriented from a super busy lifestyle, and somehow just getting by.

Of course it's hip to blame the corporations, man. But Occam's razor suggests that the simplest answer is most likely to be true; there's likely no convoluted conspiracy at play to keep the '9 to 5'. The reality is that it's hard enough to get a group of people to agree on what toppings to order on a pizza, let alone trying to get everyone to agree on a new standard working day. Until something drastic happens, like robots that can drive cars and write news articles, we need to make the most of our current system.

On the positive side, work gives many people a deep sense of identity. I have personally worked with many interesting and talented people; and I've enjoyed building relationships and learning from them. These are people who gain deep personal satisfaction from their work and related contributions to the workplace. Who hasn't heard their grumpy uncle declare—"*I'd rather die than retire!*"—after a beer or three at Thanksgiving? Some people's sense of self is so intertwined with their employment status that they'd like to be immortalized with it: "Here lies Ben—Husband, Father, and the best damn podiatrist in greater Seattle." But is it critical for people to have a sense of identity from employment?

Of course, the most reasonable response to the intense pressures of work-driven egos and time-poor lives is likely a moderate one. There is nothing wrong with choosing to work long hours every day but, like the poor factory workers before unionization, it is not necessarily sustainable. It's much easier and healthier to do so as a choice rather than as a requirement. That is why FI is goal for so many people, regardless of whether early retirement is a part of their plans.

But what is work, anyways? Is it the rudimentary exchange of time and effort for money? No - that's a job. Work is expending your physical or mental capacities towards a goal, whether in return for money or not. Even in retirement people still "work" under that definition of the word, because it's healthy and can be enjoyable if it's engaging in a creative, social, logical, or other enjoyable way. So, we'll always be working in that sense and it may even be in exchange for money.

Achieving FI makes working better in terms of your enjoyment of it but also in terms of the likely quality of your work. Lawyers that are FI may be free to take more pro-bono cases. Business owners may compensate their employees more or take extra risks in developing life changing technologies than they might otherwise. The possibilities for what you can accomplish with "work" once you're FI are endless. Work is simply better when you don't need the money.

The social commentary on this subject is nothing new and many people will be able to relate FI to the concept of "F--K you, money". This money gives you power to say no (or yes) to bosses, co-workers, and just about anyone else. Want to start working from home a couple of days a week, but the boss says no? Being FI gives you leverage to quit, negotiate harder, or find a different job with the flexibility you want. Do you want to take a six month vacation but find that the boss won't commit to hiring you back afterwards? FI allows you to take more control over the development of your career and not risk your family's security.

Everyone seeking FI will have to make a decision about retirement, whether it's early or not. It's a personal decision and I can't tell you which choice to make, but the freedom of choice sounds like a good problem to have. Personally, I know that I will continue working as long as I'm engaged and enjoying what I do.

Chapter 2

The stages of FI: Okay, okay—so, how much do I need?

There are two stages of financial independence (FI):

1. The accumulation stage: You are paying down debts, saving money, and relying on active sources of income like a job or business to cover your expenses.

2. The withdrawal stage: Your income from passive sources of investments is greater than your expenses. You could rely on those passive sources to pay for your expenses if you so choose.

Let's jump ahead and look at stage two, the withdrawal stage, because that's the exciting part and setting goals is important.

So how do we know when we're there? Is it as complicated as it seems?

Retirement planning often conjures up images of cascading spreadsheets and accountants in a race to blur the buttons on their calculators. Every financial magazine has their own way of calculating how much money you need to save up for retirement and a scary list of pitfalls and bad decisions like "10 Things This Couple Did Wrong in Their Retirement Plan!" The truth is far more simple:

you need 25 times your annual expenses to be financially independent today. It's that straight-forward. If you want an annual income of $40,000, your *FI number* should be $1,000,000. Need $20,000 a year? Your FI number is $500,000.

Now don't give up before you start. If you're thinking, "Well, that's ridiculous! I'm never going to be able to save 25 times my annual expenses," then hold onto your hat. We'll address how to get there in the next chapter. For now, let's see where that '25 times' figure comes from.

The colloquially named *"Trinity Study"* was conducted at Trinity University in 1998 in an attempt to determine a portfolio's *safe withdrawal rate* (SWR). In the study, the researchers tried to figure out the amount of money that you can take out from a bundle of investments each year without running out of funds. They tracked different investments over a 30-year period while withdrawing a set amount each year and if there was money left after 30 years, that withdrawal rate was deemed a success. The famous study spawned a rule of thumb—known as *the 4% rule*—and launched renewed academic interest into studying retirement planning and SWRs.

The study simulated (or "backtested") stock (equities) and bond data from 1925 to 1995 in 30-year intervals. There were five portfolios tested, including one which consisted of 60% stocks and 40% bonds, and one which consisted of 75% stocks and 25% bonds. With a 4% withdrawal rate, those two portfolios were successful—meaning, they didn't run out of money—more than 95% of the time. As 1 divided by 4% equals 25, this is where the '25 times' figure comes to make our FI number.

In the study, a portfolio was successful if its balance was never fully depleted, but most simulated portfolios rose way above their starting point. In over 70% of simulations, the 60% stock portfolio was worth more after 30 years than when it started, even though money was being taken out every year. This undeniable robustness is what makes the 4% rule a fantastic starting point and our rule of thumb. The 4% rule has failed, but nearly all of the failures occurred when the withdrawal stage began right before a stock market crash. But you could've guessed that. You don't need me to tell you that retiring at the end of 2008 was unlucky timing.

One great benefit of the Trinity study was the amount of attention that the topic received after it was published. Websites such as *firecalc.com* and *cfiresim.com* allow people to backtest their own investment portfolios using historical data from 1870 onwards and within any parameters they choose to set.

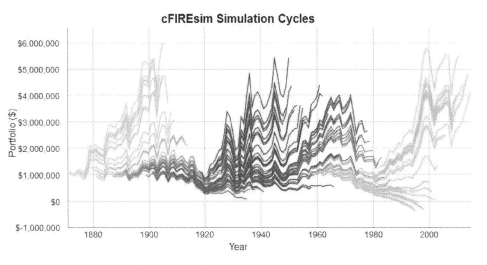

Figure 4: cFIREsim simulation cycles.

The portfolio tested above on *cfiresim.com* (see Figure 4) shows an over 95% rate of success with the following parameters:

- 1 million dollar starting portfolio and 40K annual spending (4%)

- 115 simulations of 30 year periods starting in 1871

- 60/40 split of stocks/bonds using historical returns

In the simulation, each line represents a start of the withdrawal stage. There are 115 years that were tested, so there are 115 lines on the chart. Each line begins with a balance of one million dollars on January 1st of its respective year. It is then thrown to the mercy of financial returns of days past and is subject to yearly withdrawals of $40,000. When reading Figure 4, it is less important to look at any specific line than it is to follow the volume of lines above and below $0, and the volume above and below the starting value of $1 million.

Perhaps the most important lesson from this simulation is that failed portfolios always started withdrawals at very unfortunate times, like right before the some of the larger recessions in history. The first few years of market returns, after the withdrawal stage begins, can make or break the success of a portfolio and clearly signal if your portfolio is one of the unlucky 5% that will run out of funds. This is known as the *sequence of returns risk*. In essence, in every portfolio there will be years it achieves below average returns but these will balance out with the years with above average returns. Unfortunately, the earlier in the withdrawal stage that you get those below average returns, the less likely it will be that your portfolio will be successful.

 If you are worried about that 5% chance that your portfolio will run out of money, consider that it's more likely your portfolio will triple in value than go below the zero line. Simply look at the volume of lines above $3 million compared to the volume of lines that hit $0! Of course no withdrawal plan or percentage, like anything in life, is 100% guaranteed. These past results are a useful planning tool, but your future results won't match them exactly. It's also important to note that equities and bonds are in no way the only route to FI; merely a popular one. We'll talk about ways to increase that 95% chance of success, other SWR percentages, and routes other than stocks and bonds, later on.

Since publication, the Trinity study has spawned a lot of debate centered on the practicality and real-life feasibility of the 4% rule for individual investors; what if you live to be 130 because of future medical advances? Basing your withdrawal stage on a 30-year simulation would seem awfully short-sighted in light of this futuristic possibility. What happens if your spending varies more significantly, year to year, than predicted? Will the 4% rule hold up over uncertain future economic times? How do we account for unknown healthcare costs and government pensions in old age?

These concerns are certainly valid but they can all be overcome. Let's discuss them later and agree for now that having '25 times your annual expenses' is a fantastic place to start working towards FI.

The power of saving

So, there it is. A simple formula for FI. Maybe you've been to countless advisors, read dozens of news articles, and heard all the hot tips from your neighbour about how to make it to retirement—but now you've finally found it. That magical number is rudely, or maybe even aggressively, staring right at you, but don't look away! If you are sitting there and wondering how the hell you are going to save up 25 times what you spend each year, then you're not alone. I can hear it: "Oh that's the big secret, just save a ridiculously huge amount of money," you collectively groaned as you strained your eye muscles in a record-breaking group eye roll. The good news is that you don't have to save 25 times your current annual expenses to *get* 25 times your annual expenses. You have two powerful tools to make saving towards your FI possible: investment income and your savings rate.

First, let's talk about investment income. The power of compound returns is simply laid out in the opening joke about cigarettes but just because it's a punch line doesn't make it any less effective. Compound returns means that your returns (dividends, interest, or capital gains) start earning returns themselves. Think of it as your savings account earning interest, and then that interest earning more interest, and so on.

The FI number gives you a goal to shoot for, but you'll get there by saving and investing say, 12-16 times your annual spending, not the full 25 times. Your investment income, through the power of compound returns, will earn you money that will put you the rest of the way to your FI number.

Let's illustrate investment income by looking at someone who wants a crazily extravagant lifestyle in FI. They want to spend $70,000 in a year, or more than *twice* the median American income. Using the 4% rule, this person needs to have $1.75 million invested in a 60/40 mix of stocks and bonds similar to the portfolio described in the Trinity study above. For illustration purposes, let's assume they invest $30,000 a year and make a 6% return on average after inflation, for 25 years. (A 6% real return rate is reasonable, if conservative, for what we can expect over a long period of time, but we'll talk more about that later.) For now, let's make the assumption and look at Figure 5.

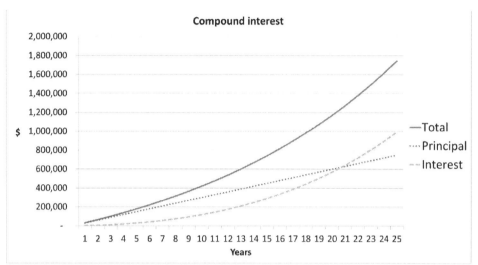

Figure 5: The effect of compound returns (in this case, interest) on total balance. Make similar calculations by searching for a compound interest calculator.

The outcome from this calculation is clear: without saving even half of that juicy $1.75 million portfolio this lavishly rich individual could be able to meet their extravagant FI goal. In fact, they only saved $750,000, or 43% of the portfolio's final balance, and the rest of it was earned through compound returns, shown as interest in the graph above. The snowball effect of compound interest where investing money earns money, which is then in turn earning even more money, is a powerful phenomenon that greatly decreases the time it takes to gain financial independence.

In order to get compounding on your side, you need to start investing as early as you can. The snowball effect follows an exponential curve and takes time to start to work for you. But don't fret if you haven't started yet. Although the best time to start investing was yesterday, or 20 years ago, the second best time is *right now*.

The second most powerful tool available to drastically decrease your time to financial independence is your savings rate; and more specifically, finding ways to increase it! Don't know what your monthly savings rate is? Calculating it is simple: take your after-tax income (from your pay checks) and subtract your expenses. The amount left over equals your savings. Then, your savings divided by your after-tax income equals your savings rate.

If you have no idea what your savings rate is, and can't imagine yourself actually breaking out the calculator to figure it out, you'll want to rethink that stance after you see this next figure because it turns out that your savings rate is the fastest and easiest way to estimate your time to FI. Figure 6 shows the impact of savings rates on FI (generated with data from *http://networthify.com*) based on a modest 5% average return.

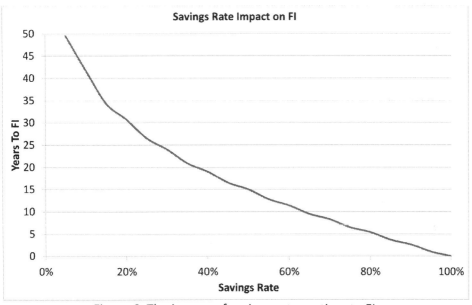

Figure 6: The impact of savings rate on time to FI.

You may notice that the relationship between your savings rate and the number of years until FI is not linear. If you are currently on the far left of this graph, you can see that making what might seem like a token effort to save some money can be immensely powerful. To illustrate how small changes can be impactful, consider how increasing your savings rate from 10% to 15% decreases your time to FI by 8 years, whereas an increase from 40% to 45% only decreases your time by 3 years. If you aren't saving anything right now, let this chart be an incentive to get you kick-started and on your way to FI.

Increasing your savings rate is incredibly powerful because it highlights the impact of decreasing your expenses. Like a double whammy, decreasing your expenses not only gives you more money to invest right now, it also eliminates the need to pay for those expenses in the future. Think about it this way: let's say that you pay $500 every year for hair appointments. You'll need to create a fund of 25 times that amount—so $12,500—to pay for that expense every year. Now that's quite a bit of money to save for your hair so you decide to spend only $300 per year. This small reduction not only gives you an extra $200 a year extra to invest towards your goal of $12,500, it actually decreases the goal of $12,500 itself. Now, at $300 per year, the goal to create a hair care perpetuity fund is only $7,500 (or $300 X 25). That should be a lot easier to accomplish with an extra $200 a year in your pocket!

Figure 7: A '25 times' fund for each expense in the withdrawal stage.

People like to compare savings rates and it is true that they can be a good indicator of someone's dedication to achieving FI. However, people not only vary in their income levels but also in their calculation methods, so don't get too caught up in other rate formulas. The most important number is your savings rate and its movement over time. Calculate your savings rate using a consistent formula to make sure you're staying on track and hitting your goal.

Figure 6 is a great visual reminder of what saving can do for you, but after you've nailed down a budget and saving has become second nature to you, your savings rate calculation becomes less meaningful. It will still remind you of how much you're saving compared to other months in the past, but it won't tell you how much further you have to go to get to your FI number. At this point, tracking your net worth and the value of your investments will more accurately allow you to estimate your time to FI as you get closer to the finish line.

Experiment and find the right savings rate for you. Push the boundaries and look for that sweet spot where you can live a content and fulfilled life while maximizing your savings rate, but don't forget to keep some perspective. As George Carlin once joked about highway driving, "everyone going slower than you is an idiot, and everyone going faster than you is a maniac!" This is just as true for FI—not everyone saving more than you must be a miserable hermit person, and not everyone saving less than you is an idiotic, consumption-happy zombie. Be open to others' viewpoints and above all, be kind to one another.

The link between money and happiness

What's the point of saving up all this money for some far off future if you're never going to enjoy it on the journey, right? Life is short, and you work hard. Don't you deserve nice things? And those nice things will make you happy, right?

Maybe buying a brand new SUV every few years makes you happy. And if you can afford it, why shouldn't you indulge yourself? You tell yourself that there's nothing like that new car smell and testing the limits of your new German-made engine. You feel amazing rolling around in your shiny new wheels. Or at least until the smell wears off and you find out how rarely to you get to rev up that engine when you're stuck in rush hour traffic. In the span of a few short months, you find that your fancy new portable living room (complete with a heated steering wheel and TV in the back) has reverted back to just being "the car."

Does this sound familiar?

In their study titled *Lottery Winners And Accident Victims: Is Happiness Relative (1978)*[2], Brickman, Coates, and Janoff-Bulman found that spikes and dips in happiness—as reported by lottery winners and newly handicapped people—revert back to a baseline relatively quickly. As you might guess, after tracking happiness levels over time, the authors found that new lottery winners were exceedingly happy right after their big win and newly paraplegic people were incredibly distraught after their injury. Unexpected, however, was how quickly both groups returned to their "pre-incident" level of happiness. Indeed, within just *two months*, both groups were largely back to being at happiness levels similar to those reported before their windfalls or accidents.

Follow up studies in the 21st century are conflicted on whether big, once in a lifetime events can permanently change your baseline happiness or not. (The consensus so far is 'no' for marriage and 'yes' for incarceration.) But they all agree that relatively smaller events like cutting cable TV, losing your job, and even buying that new car, can only temporarily change your happiness levels. In addition, as noted by Lucas, Clark, Georgellis, & Diener (2003) in *Reactions to Changes in Marital Status*[3], individuals appear to have different levels of adaptability and some are more likely than others to return to a baseline level of happiness. Keep in mind that these studies were usually conducted on people with no history of depression; people with mental ailments can permanently overcome them and raise their baseline happiness levels.

Now, how does happiness relate to your savings rate and FI? Although it's good to know that time can truly heal—whether it be a life-changing injury, or a relationship or a job loss—this human tendency can be particularly obstructive to achieving FI. It might not be obvious, but the downside of reverting to a mean

---

[2]
http://pages.ucsd.edu/~nchristenfeld/Happiness_Readings_files/Class%203%20-%20Brickman%201978.pdf
[3] http://www.apa.org/pubs/journals/releases/psp-843527.pdf

happiness baseline is that by connecting consumption with happiness, people can get trapped on the appropriately termed *hedonic treadmill*.

The classic example of the hedonic treadmill is depicted by the couple who "needs" to buy a new house every couple of years, proclaiming each time that the new one is their "dream home." We'll go over why regular real estate transactions are one of the worst financial mistakes you can make later, but for now let's examine this couple's impulses. If we were a fly on their wall, we would see them rushing around chasing the adrenaline high that lasts a few short months after buying a new house. Each house is bigger and has a better view than the last, but eventually their new house will start to feel a bit rag-tag and they will begin the cycle anew. "I don't know how we used to live like that," they might joke to each other. But what has really changed? It is most likely that nothing has really changed and they are just as happy now as they were before, except now they have more material 'stuff.'

Here's another example: a co-worker of mine came in to work each morning with a luxurious and freshly brewed cappuccino from a local roaster. When I casually asked him how much it cost, he replied that not only did he not know, he didn't care. Having a luxury coffee each morning made him happy, he insisted. Much happier, he argued, than the free coffee offered at the office. For him, it was worth it to spend a couple of bucks on an item that made coming into work so much more palatable.

Figure 8: "The latte effect" is a cliché in personal finance books, but that doesn't make it any less legitimate... You'll forgive me eventually.

Now, I agree with my co-worker. Coffee is nice! Especially those locally brewed cappuccinos. But I disagree with him on just *how* nice they are. I estimated that his $5 per workday, or $100 per month habit represented about 3.5% of his monthly after-tax income. If he was already saving 10% of his after-tax income, skipping those fancy drinks would get him to FI almost *6 years faster*. And I agree that those cappuccinos taste much better than our office coffee, maybe even twice as good, but I don't agree that they're *that* good. The obvious irony is that the very thing that was helping him get through his monotonous, boring office day was actually keeping him there much longer than he'd have guessed.

Needless to say, after our conversation, he enjoys the office coffee much more now that he's moving faster towards financial independence.

Psychologically, my co-worker didn't actually enjoy the boutique coffee. He enjoyed the rush of endorphins that he got when he spent money on something. The act of buying got his adrenaline and dopamine pumping through his brain and gave him a habit-forming high that he "needed" to start his work day. In short, like many of us, he was addicted to spending money. It may not seem like it, but saving money towards FI is also spending money, except instead of a material gain, you're buying time. Delaying your gratification for trivial possessions is certainly a good trade for the ability to be in complete control of your life.

Occasionally, the urge to buy those fancy cappuccinos still comes over my co-worker and me. It's human nature to crave things that give you instant satisfaction. After all, our ancient ancestors had no guarantee that food wouldn't spoil or be stolen by predators in the middle of the night. It was safer for cavemen to gorge themselves when they could. As a result, it is difficult for humans to prioritize long-term strategies over immediately gratifying impulses, and the path to financial independence is one long haul.

The good news is that we are not cavemen and we've learned a lot about ourselves since those days. The bad news is that we are still tempted by the same impulses and marketers have learned how to exploit this weakness with flashing lights and instant credit everywhere we go. The solution is to arm ourselves with awareness. Any time I find myself salivating over an impulse buy, whether big or small, I remind myself, "Scientists have already figured this stuff out, stupid!" Delaying gratification allows you to make that more thoughtful decision towards financial independence and the meaningful and long-term happiness that FI can give you. There's no need to deny that those cravings for the hottest brand name clothes exist but it's helpful to put them into perspective.

Avoiding rash and emotional decisions can literally shave years off your required work life. Let the reward chemicals in your brain settle down. If it still looks like a good buy after some rational thought and waiting, then go for it. You'll be surprised by just how many things you no longer need or want after a two-week freeze out period. Some people implement a sliding scale system based on dollar amounts. For every hundred or thousand dollars a purchase might cost, that adds an extra day or week to their waiting period before they make a purchase. Although it's difficult, you'll eventually adapt to new habits like this one and return to a baseline level of happiness. The hedonic treadmill will make sure of it.

Financial independence doesn't have to be about being a hermit and early retiring at twenty to a shack in the countryside. It's not even about being extremely cheap or frugal. FI is about maximizing your happiness by balancing your spending and savings and fully understanding the impact of your major financial decisions. Nobody likes a cheapskate. Don't avoid buying snacks for the kids at your daughter's birthday party but do question the marginal happiness that a 6-year-old receives from a $1,000 birthday party compared to a $200 birthday party.

Although denying a 6-year-old a four-figure birthday party fit for a real princess seems like a logical and easy thing to do, the choices get more difficult when we consider our own indulgences and hobbies. A friend of mine was recently very excited about starting his journey to FI until I discovered that he was spending over $1,000 a month on a competitive, collectible card game. This game, although expensive, was one of his main sources of social interaction and fun. It was difficult and took time but my friend finally admitted to himself that he would be equally as happy if he focused on his other hobbies, including hiking and less expensive card games. He's now liquidated and invested his "shrine to materialism," or $40,000 card collection, and that money is out earning him a return instead of sitting in a safe.

After all that, there will still be those of you out there who would only give up your yearly BMW habit "over your dead body," and that's okay as long as you've really thought about the quality and nature of the happiness that the BMW brings you and have made peace with the consequential delay to FI that it brings.

Let's be clear: there is nothing disingenuous about encouraging people to save money for their future happiness while simultaneously saying that money can't buy happiness. Financial independence and happiness are closely related because being FI, or even having a FI mindset, allows you to deliberately focus on the sources of happiness in your life. Achieving FI boils down to three steps:

1. Spending money can't make you happy. (Remember the dangers of the hedonic treadmill.)
2. In order to be free from worrying about money, you will need a lot of it.
3. Focus on that which brings you real happiness and make decisions to achieve FI.

Remember, we all agreed that FI was a worthwhile, respectable, and achievable goal for the majority of the developed world. But how fast you get there is up to you. What may appear like excessive materialism to you could be another person's honest attempt at cutting back on luxury goods and finding the balance that is right for them.

Dealing with debt

The amount of non-mortgage debt that the average person carries has exploded in the last 10 years. This is particularly true for young people as the skyrocketing costs of higher education have left many with hundreds of thousands in student debt. Low interest rates have also had an intoxicating effect for many. The cheaper it gets to borrow money, the more people will do it. If you're fortunate enough to have no non-mortgage debt, feel free to skip this section.

If you do have non-mortgage debt, take solace in the fact that you're not alone. It's a challenge faced by many and it's important to acknowledge that it is a significant psychological challenge. Debt can feel overwhelming, like walking around with a weight on your shoulders. Take a deep breath because you're on course to overcome this challenge and be on your way to FI. First you have to get in the right headspace: know that debt doesn't define you as a human being. In fact, money doesn't make anyone a good, bad, generous, or evil person. So let's meet this challenge with a clear mind and the motivation to win.

You'll have to treat debt seriously if you want to stop it from slowly bleeding you out financially. Yes, in this day and age it may seem normal to have a lot of debt but treating debt as such is one way to ensure you'll never get out of it. Every time you catch yourself window shopping, you should have air horns going off inside of your head. Neon signs should be flashing in your mind when you get the urge to buy something superfluous. It sounds simple but if you want to pay off your debt quickly, something most people can't or won't do, you'll need a different approach and mindset from most people.

In order to beat your debt, you're going to have to treat it like the emergency that it is. Compound interest—the force that makes saving and investing so powerful—works against you if you have debt. And guess what: it doesn't care about where you got it from. Whether you borrowed money for school or to fund a high stakes poker game, compound interest will continue to pile-up against you, growing ever larger, compounding every month until you are afraid to open the bill. It's a runaway snowball; a cancerous growth.

Now that you're ready to tackle your debt, make a list of all your loans and note where they came from, their interest rates, and any other penalties they might be waiting to spring on you. Staying organized and watching the amounts you owe go down over time will keep you motivated. Make sure that you legally need to pay each of the loans you've listed. Maybe someone with a similar name has taken out a loan and the collection agency is confused. Or maybe the loan is so old that it's past the statute of limitations in your area. Look it up as each region has different amounts of time for which you are legally required to pay the money back. Perhaps there's someone else who was a co-signer on your loan and they also owe the money. Whatever you need to do, figure out the details and write it down. Gathering up all this information is vital so that you can establish the big picture and set realistic timelines as goals for paying each loan off.

Next, you can try different ways to reduce the amounts that you owe. Negotiation can pay off well and you may even want to hire someone to do this for you. Credit card companies in particular may give you a lower interest rate if you call and ask for it. Sometimes just asking to cut a deal and reduce the amount that you owe can actually work. Creditors would rather get half of what you owe them than none at all, so it never hurts to ask. Another great idea is refinancing or consolidating your debts into one loan with a lower interest rate.

By taking out a line of credit or home equity line of credit and paying off your credit cards and other debt with it, you may be able to drastically reduce the amount you'll pay over the long-term.

There are two main approaches to actually paying off debt: the snowball method and the avalanche method. The snowball method starts with paying off the loans with the smallest dollar amounts owing first. The idea is that you'll get a psychological feeling of accomplishment by paying off those small loans, and it will give you the motivation you need to keep going. When your smallest loan is paid off, the payments you made every month to it are added to the minimum payments of the next smallest loan, resulting in you making bigger and bigger payments, like a snowball.

The avalanche approach will help you get out of debt and achieve FI faster because it works by paying off the loan with the highest interest rate first. The math is simple: by getting rid of your highest interest rate loans first you will pay less total interest over time. If you have the mental fortitude needed to go with the avalanche approach, you should definitely go with this option.

Paying off debt is a double-whammy. By getting used to setting aside money each month to pay your debt, you'll have good habits in place for when you pay it off and start building your savings. You'll change those monthly loan payments to savings and you'll be on your way to achieving FI! Everyone wants to pay off debt faster, or save more, but there's no magic bullet. You either need to spend less or earn more—those are your only options. It's kind of like losing weight: you can only do it by expending more calories with a workout or by taking in fewer calories. There isn't a lot of room for innovative techniques regardless of what the commercials say.

Later, we'll talk about cutting your spending to a rate that will give you an acceptable debt-payoff date, or FI date, by designing a budget.

Chapter 3

Should you trust the stock market?

Is all this talk about investing making you anxious? Maybe the elephant in the room is actually the fickle boogeyman of capitalism – the stock market. If the thought of Wall Street traders shouting over each other and pulling their hair is giving you heart palpitations, take some deep breaths. Then remember that the best way to get over a phobia is through direct exposure. And in this case, that's exactly what the doctor is ordering.

Figure 9: Apply twice daily.

So, what exactly is the stock market? It's a 'marketplace' where you can buy ownership of a company called "equity." And equity is a very powerful tool, buying stocks and owning shares in a company allows you to vote on important issues and receive a portion of the profits made by the company. As a shareholder, you expect to receive profits in return for the money you've invested and the employees of the company work to make this happen. Stocks aren't just numbers on a screen. They aren't a mysterious black box. Stocks represent real people doing real things for their employers and shareholders.

The stock market is not the same as 'the economy'. The stock market allows investors to set their expectations for the performance of a company by negotiating prices for pieces of those companies; in contrast, the economy is more broadly defined as a system that facilitates the production, consumption, and distribution of finite resources. In fact, the stock market is just one example of an indicator used to analyze the performance of the economy. Other economic indicators include the unemployment rate, retail sales, and the number of houses under construction in a given period of time. The stock market is a *leading indicator* and its performance can be used to predict future changes in the overall economy. Because it represents investor expectations of future profit, a general rise in stock prices means that the economy is likely to follow it. Interest rates set by central bankers and the unemployment rate are *lagging or coincident indicators* and they change after, or at the same time as, the overall economy.

Notice how the stock market is different from gold or real estate. Metal doesn't know what you want from it. It's not out there every day trying to make money for you. And many don't want to, or don't have the skill set that's needed to work with passive sources of income such as those from a small business or rental property. We'll talk about real estate later, as it's definitely a valid route to FI, but being a landlord is not a fit for everyone. If that's true for you, stock and bond investments (*securities*) are a great investment option to achieve your passive income source. And that's exactly what we're going to do, invest—not gamble—our way to financial independence.

So, how much money do our investments need to return in order to get us to Fi? The Trinity study used historical data to simulate stock and bond portfolios over 30-year periods. In most 30-year periods, equity markets (or stocks) gave their owners an average of 7% real return per year. *Real return* is the monetary payout of an investment after accounting for inflation, and in financial independence, you need to out-earn inflation as well as your annual withdrawals. That's right; the 4% safe withdrawal rate (SWR) is reliant not only on you investing in equities, but on those equities returning 7% after inflation on average. Are you sweating yet? Let's look at why it may not be such a crazy assumption.

The stock market: A case for rational optimism

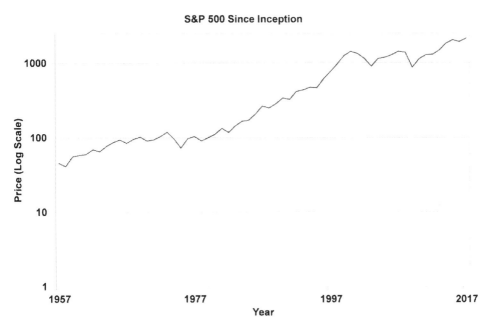

Figure 10: Logarithmic chart of the S&P 500 since inception.

The *S&P 500* is composed America's 500 largest stocks. To give you some perspective, Figure 10 charts out the collective returns of the S&P 500 from 1957 to 2016 on a logarithmic scale. Can you see the great dips on the graph of the 2008 housing market collapse and subsequent "great recession"? It felt epic at the time, but is it in the big picture? If you examine the graph carefully, you will see that in fact, every decade had at least one crisis moment when the stock markets took a big hit. Need a few examples to jog your memory?

From late 1969 to the early 1970, inflation hit 7% as the Vietnam War raged. Stocks fell over 35% from their peak, causing widespread panic and fear. Less than four years later, unemployment reached 9% and inflation reached double digits, sending a reeling stock market down 50% over the course of six months. And don't forget "the crash of '87" where we saw stocks drop down 23% in one day for no reason other than investor-fear and panicked sales. And then there was the summer of 1998, when Russia defaulted on its debt and nearly brought down numerous Wall St. banks. Of course, that was quickly forgotten a few years later when the "dot-com bubble" burst and the 9/11 terrorist attacks stifled business activity. Post-9/11, stocks dropped a further 49%.

Now pull back a bit and you'll see that even amid this constant chaos and turmoil, the S&P 500 is up, overall, 1,100-fold since World War 2. The media would have us all believe that we need to make a choice: optimists vs. pessimists, bears vs. bulls, but these are false dichotomies. There's a third, less vocal group made up of long-term optimists who expect bumps—or even cliffs—along the way. It's not a matter of *if* there will be another recession or stock market downturn because there *will* be one at some point. What's important is that we learn from the past and invest in a way that doesn't compromise our individual financial goals.

Panic still seems to be part of the stock market today. Current investors are losing their hats over concerns about China's slowing growth rates and a glut of oil flooding the market due to advances in shale drilling technology in the southern United States. TV personalities are screaming that the S&P 500 is going to end up 75% lower in 2016 than it started and that we'll all be living in caves before long.

For us who know that the long-term trend of the market is upwards, it's impossible to see these minor drops as anything other than a buying opportunity. When you are investing for financial independence (FI), you are investing for the long term. So, if you have hope that humans will continue to thrive as a species and that technology will continue to propel us forward, then you should have no qualms about investing for the long-term.

And what if the worst-case scenario were to occur, and we ended up back in caves using bottle caps as currency? There's always the looming threat of some rogue state getting its hands on a nuclear weapon, or the entire monetary system of the world collapsing like a house of cards for some unpredictable reason. I can't promise that the next president won't press the big red button but I do know that at that point it won't matter much. Under those dire conditions, regardless of how many luxury cars were bought or the balance of one's retirement investments, we will all meet the same fate.

If you've been paying attention, you might realize that the principles of FI fit well with the principles of economic stewardship. That's no mistake. Living a materialistic existence isn't just bad for your wallet; it's bad for our collective continued existence on Earth. In 2013, 97% of actively publishing scientists collectively declared that it was extremely likely that man-made climate change is a real threat to the Earth and the well-being of all life. Living a conscientious ethos and a low-carbon lifestyle can also help you on your way to FI.

Climate change is the most realistic large scale threat to humanity. Everybody should be doing what they can to combat this problem, but we'll discuss the merits of socially responsible investing in Appendix A: Green funds and fossil fuel divestment. I don't pretend to know the effect that climate change will have on global equities, but I hope it won't be worse than any of the wars and crises the world has seen since the stock market came into existence.

So when is the right time to invest? The answer is always "as soon as possible." It doesn't matter if the stock market appears to be at a relative high point with no indication of a coming drop. In fact, the stock market should routinely hit all-time highs due to inflation. Of course, don't tell the media that the next time they run a panicked cover story about a new high posted by the Dow Jones or S&P 500. Better yet, try to avoid all day-to-day media noise about the stock market. Sensationalism and empirical evidence doesn't mix well when you're trying to make solid investment decisions.

One common debate I frequently encounter is whether it's better to invest your money through *dollar cost averaging*, i.e. spread out over time, or immediately as a lump sum once it is available. The difference is that investors following the *lump sum approach* would invest right when they receive the funds whereas investors using an averaging method would wait and spread out that investment over several weeks or months.

Due to the upwards trend of the stock market in the 20th century, it should be no surprise to you that a study's findings titled *Dollar-Cost Averaging Just Means Taking Risk Later*[4] found lump sum approach came out ahead about two thirds

---

[4] https://pressroom.vanguard.com/nonindexed/7.23.2012_Dollar-cost_Averaging.pdf

of the time. The study, conducted by a popular ETF and index fund provider, is inherently biased towards you investing your money and doing it sooner rather than later. But their approach and conclusions are accurate. The only benefit of dollar-cost averaging is that it allows you to defer risk. By holding onto cash for longer, you decrease the size of the shock you'll get if your investments unluckily plummet in value right after your purchase. If you're investing for the short-term, then there's an argument to be made for this kind of approach. But if you are investing for the short-term, you should consider avoiding equities altogether. Money that needs to be accessed in a short time period (e.g. less than 3 years) is generally better off in less risky investments like bonds or in a savings account.

In order to reap the advantages of long-term economic prosperity, you need to be able to stomach the occasional sharp drop in order to avoid selling at a loss. Unfortunately, most big stock drops coincide with high unemployment levels and you won't be able to hold onto your investments if you need to sell them to put food on the table. In order to ensure that you won't have to sell low, the first thing you're going to do on the path to FI is to create an emergency fund. A comprehensive emergency fund is enough money to cover 3+ months of expenses and is stashed in a high interest savings account in case you lose your job. You can increase or decrease this amount depending on how stable your job is, or you can even use a line of credit. This will help you to ride out a recession and let you stay fully invested in the stock market during any downturns.

Another powerful tool to avoid selling equities at a loss is re-balancing, which we'll discuss shortly. We'll also talk more about steps to take after creating an emergency fund and the peak doom phenomenon of endless end-of-times predictions.

The merits of financial advisors: I need an adult!

Are you wondering, why not just use a financial advisor to figure all this stuff out? Wouldn't it help you rest easier if a professional was looking after your money in a safe mutual fund? The short answer is no; you definitely should not use a financial advisor unless you want to add significantly to the number of years it will take for you to become financially independent (FI). And as you will see, the rationale is 'short and sweet.'

As we learned above, the S&P 500 has achieved 7% real returns since its inception and investors always have the option of buying an index fund that tracks indices including the S&P 500. An *index fund* is a type of mutual fund that holds thousands of stocks inside of it but it is passively managed. In contrast, the traditional mutual fund is actively managed by an advisor who chooses the stocks in the fund. There is no adviser or manager of an index fund and the fund simply holds each stock in the index at its relative size, or *market cap*. For example, if company A issued 100 shares of stock worth $2 each, its market cap would be $200. And if the total market cap of all of the stocks on the market totaled $10,000, then 2% (200/10,000) of the stocks within an index fund would be Company A's stock. Oh, and the most important part—passive index funds often *cost 10 times less* than similar mutual funds!

In order for a financial advisor (or mutual fund manager) to be worth the added cost, they would need to be able to beat an index, like the S&P 500, on a regular basis by at least as much as their fees. Unfortunately, study after study has shown that these "experts" are unable to outperform the market (usually the S&P 500) on a consistent basis regardless of the type of investment, be it individual stocks or mutual funds.

But there must be some good mutual fund managers out there, right? Wrong! The majority of mutual fund managers aren't able to beat the index that they are judged against. Their inability to provide superior returns has been proven by academics *many*[5], *many*[6], *many*[7] times over. In 2014, *86%*[8] of mutual fund managers couldn't beat the market. And that's before they took their commissions! Now, 2014 was not just a chance bad year for fund managers.

---

[5] http://web.stanford.edu/~wfsharpe/art/active/active.htm
[6] us.spindices.com/documents/spiva/spiva-us-year-end-2012.pdf?force_download=true
[7] https://papers.ssrn.com/sol3/papers.cfm?abstract_id=869748
[8] http://money.cnn.com/2015/03/12/investing/investing-active-versus-passive-funds/

From 2004 to 2014—that's ten years—82% of managers underperformed their indices and a good chunk of those that did beat their indices did so out of sheer luck. How's that for peace of mind?

So why are all of these "professional investors" so bad at picking stocks? A large part of it has to do with the *efficient market hypothesis*, a concept developed by Nobel Laureate Eugene Fama in the 1960s. The hypothesis proposes that, at any point in time, all or most information known by the public about a particular stock is already factored into its share price. The revelation of this hypothesis is the implication that stocks always trade at their fair value; meaning that they cost what they are truly worth.

Theoretically, if the market was efficient, it would be impossible for any investor to out-perform the market—with two-caveats. The first is that the market is only efficient in the long run. In any given year an investor could get lucky and beat the market. It's beating the market consistently which is so difficult. The second is that an investor can also beat the market if they take on more risk than the average company in the market. We'll talk more about risk-adjusted returns later but for now, let's accept that good research—like the follow up study by *Fama & French in 2009*[9]—confirms that using a mutual fund manager is about just as good of an idea as throwing darts at a board to pick your stocks.

So, how do the advisors choose which stocks to include in their funds? There are two main types of analysis: *fundamental* and *technical*. Fundamental analysis primarily involves analyzing a company's financial statements and other financial information to find the underlying value of a company. Technical analysis prioritizes data and predicting stock price movement based on trends. We won't need to discuss these types of analysis any further, because they're used for picking individual stocks and don't relate to the broad based index approach supported by this book.

But before advisors start technical or fundamental analysis, they first need to find out what the market thinks of a company. Let's look at a company that is frequently speculated on, like Tesla. Everyone knows that their products are hot. Demand is so high that they can't keep the cars on their lots for more than

---

[9] https://papers.ssrn.com/sol3/papers.cfm?abstract_id=1356021

a couple days. So, what factors affect the company's share price? One of the most important is the company's ability to make enough cars to meet demand without sacrificing profits—in other words, supply. The limiting factor of Tesla's 2015 supply chain was the source and production of lithium-ion for their batteries and yet in 2015, they delivered 50,000 Model S vehicles. Industry analysts think they'll be able to deliver anywhere from 60,000 to 80,000 cars in 2016.

Like human analysts, the non-sentient market acts like it has expectations of how many cars Tesla will supply in the next quarter or year. And each price point has built in expectations of exactly how many cars they'll be able to sell. If the company beats the market expectations for number of cars, the stock price is likely to rise, and vice versa if the company is wrong. When investors try to beat the market, they first trying to understand what the market is expecting from a stock and then trying to determine if the stock will beat those expectations.

Phew! We haven't even considered the impact of expenses or oil prices and I'm already exhausted!

Opponents of this theory argue that humans are irrational and make emotional decisions regarding their investments. They point to random fluctuations in stock prices without changes in the underlying fundamentals of a company as proof and they are right. In the short-term, stocks bounce up and down by the second with absolutely no new information being released to the public. That is because on a day-to-day basis, the stock market acts like a betting machine for people to vote for stocks that they expect to be favoured, or unfavoured, in the next piece of news. It is only in the long-run that the stock market acts like a scale that tips towards—or gives relatively more value—to companies that have experienced more good news than others.

Perhaps the most famous analogy that compares how the market values companies in the short term versus the long term is Andrew Hallam's dog walking analogy. In it, the owner represents a company's true underlying value, and the dog on the leash represents that company's stock price. In the course of the walk, the dog often falls behind or runs ahead of its owner (and yes, some dogs have much longer leashes than others) but when they end their walk at home, the dog and owner are side-by-side. In the long run, the price of a stock will always reflect what it is really worth and not the day-to-day emotions of investors.

The reality is that no one—not you, me, nor your fancy financial advisor—are able to out-predict the general public consistently. Given this truth, how much value are those fancy advisors giving you? Let's break down the math for a person who wants to become financially independent with $1.5 million dollars:

Fund Comparison	Fund A - Do It Yourself	Fund B - Fancy Mutual Fund
Yearly Contribution	25,000	25,000
Average Return Per Year	7%	7%
Management Fee Percentage	.20%	3%
# of Years	25	25
Future Account Value ($)	1,535,000	1,040,000
Management Expense ($)	30,000	400,000
Lost Earnings ($)	15,000	140,000

Figure 11: The hidden expenses and opportunity cost of financial advisors.

Fund A is an index fund that we can expect to grow 7% on average, and although there are no active managers, the fund administrators charge a 0.2% annual fee to track the underlying index. Fund B is a mutual fund with 3% fees, which is about the average in North America for actively managed funds. Although we know mutual fund advisors are likely to underperform compared to the market, we'll give them the benefit of the doubt that they'll also be able to achieve 7% yearly growth. Once you look at the details, 3% fees may sound pretty measly but over the course of 25 years it adds up to roughly $400,000 in management expenses. We haven't even included the *opportunity cost*—the return that those management fees paid would have earned had they been invested—of active management here. That's another $140,000 which, I imagine if you are reading this advice, isn't exactly chump change to you.

Are you currently investing in 'fancy' mutual funds like the one shown above? If so, you shouldn't sleep soundly. You should be tossing and turning with anxiety! That small 2-3% fee that you glance over in the glossy, professional looking reports that your financial advisor sends you is costing you hundreds of thousands of dollars and years added to your working life. The investor who chooses Fund B takes almost *nine additional years* to get to their goal of $1.5 million dollars. It's time to bite the bullet and fire your financial advisor. It'll be the easiest money-making decision that you will ever make.

Advisors and mutual funds: Am I an idiot?

Feel like an idiot? You're not. Even if you're reading this from your hospital bed after a heart attack from calculating a decade of fees, don't beat yourself up. For a long time, expensive mutual funds were the only way that individual investors like you and I could get instant *diversification* of hundreds of companies. Low cost, index-tracking *exchange traded funds* (ETFs) have only achieved widespread acclaim and adoption in the past 10-15 years in the United States. Canada has fared significantly worse. Only now are Canadian banks and investment companies starting to pay attention to customers' demand for low-fee products and our mutual fund fees have always been up to a whole percent more than our American counterparts.

Or, are you still in denial? Are you asking yourself, how could all of those people, and hundreds of millions of dollars earned, be wrong? Please don't appeal to the majority; just because everyone is doing it, doesn't make it right. Your advisor is probably very well-educated and a pleasant person but unfortunately they are, at best, willfully ignorant. Turning a blind eye tends to happen when your paychecks are dependent on not seeing what's right in front of your eyes.

The actively managed fund industry has an expansive history and is deeply ingrained into the economy as a whole. Accountants, insurance brokers, and other professionals still refer clients to, and get referrals from, money managers. And that will take a long time to stop, if it even ever does. So no, you're not an idiot. At the very least, you're an informed person who is aware that you are spending unnecessarily.

After all this, if you are still clinging to the feel-good pandering that comes from using an advisor, do yourself one favour: get a promise of *fiduciary duty*. Fiduciary duty protects you with the explicit promise of the highest standard of care possible and a legal duty to always act solely in another party's (that is, your) interests. For example, if you have a lawyer, they owe you a fiduciary duty. If someone is handling your money, it is completely reasonable to expect that they do so in your best interest.

So, it is unfortunate then that many financial advisors in North America do not legally owe their clients fiduciary duty. This is a complex issue to navigate and it depends on the province or state that you live in, as well as the specific qualifications held by the advisor. It's easiest just to ask your advisor if they owe you a fiduciary duty. If they say that they don't, or can't, then they are glorified salespeople and you should walk out that door. If they do, then ask them to give you a promise of fiduciary duty in writing.

But better yet, you should run far, far away and do your own investing.

Index funds vs. ETFs vs. Mutual funds—wait, what?

Above, we discussed the studies which proved how it is impossible for financial advisors and active fund managers to beat the stock market, which is in turn made up of various indexes. And indexes are better than individual stocks because, to paraphrase John Bogle, rather than looking for the needle in the haystack, it benefits investors to just buy the entire haystack. Practically speaking, most people gain exposure to indexes through *exchange traded funds* (ETFs) because they generally have lower fees and can be bought during normal trading hours unlike mutual funds or index funds. They trade on stock exchanges –hence the name, *exchange traded funds*- which means they are easy to buy. Even better, many brokers don't charge commissions for ETF purchases.

Is your head swimming yet? Let's back up a bit and review some terms. Here are three definitions you need to know:

Figure 12: Index funds are a type of mutual fund. Exchange trade funds are another sub-set.

Mutual funds are a mixed basket of stocks, bonds, and/or other types of investment products. Traditionally, these are actively managed by professional fund administrators who might make dozens of decisions each day on what to buy and sell in order to beat other mutual funds. Mutual funds have names like

"Dynamic Global Discovery Fund" or "The Select Gold Ivy Series Premium Funds." Rule of thumb: the more ridiculous the name, the more expensive the mutual fund will be. Investments should be boring. There's no reason for your investments to sound like an advertising pitch for an outback safari vacation.

Index funds are a type of mutual fund that is passively managed and tracks an underlying index like the S&P 500 or Dow Jones. Computer systems and a small team of administrators manage index funds periodically to ensure that the funds re-balance to match their index. For example, if Apple went from being worth 4% of the NASDAQ index to being worth 5% in a single day, an index fund following the NASDAQ would buy Apple stock at the end of the day to make sure 5% of its holdings are Apple.

ETFs are another type of mutual fund. These are the easiest to buy and the cheapest to own. Unlike other mutual funds, they can be purchased through any broker because they are actually traded on the stock market. The most popular ETFs track indices like S&P 500 or the NASDAQ but they can also track specific sectors like the solar panel or consumer goods industries. For example, VTSMX, Vanguard's Total Stock Market ETF, holds shares of over 3000 companies and has an expense ratio of .16%.

Avoiding risk and controlling emotions: Can I pick my own stocks?

No. It's simply not a reasonable option.

I don't intend to sound condescending but if you have been paying attention, you'd know that even *professionals* can't consistently outperform the market. If you think that you can spend a couple of hours watching Jim Cramer on TV, or reading *Bloomberg Business,* and be able to beat the Wall Street investors then you're out of touch. In reality, beating the market requires not only grueling hard work but a lot of luck. Even with that hot tip from your uncle and a business degree, you would have to work a dozens of hours per week just to squeeze out a return that is a couple of tenths of a percent better than the overall market.

Investing for financial independence (FI) isn't about trying to make a quick buck or successfully gambling into early retirement. It's about keeping your eye on the prize—that is, building enough wealth to become FI—while you enjoy life along the way. Unless you're sure that you're the next Warren Buffet, it's time to forget what you thought you knew and focus on saving and passive income sources like index tracking ETFs or real estate.

Blindly investing in an index exchange traded fund (ETF) solely because I told you it's a decent option is a horrible idea. Education and understanding is the key to any sort of investment, or otherwise you might as well bet all your chips on red, or put all your savings into the next Enron Corp. In order to become a successful and happy investor, you'll need to be able to think like a poker player and leave your emotions, and ego, at the door because otherwise they will burn you. That's why it's important to understand why buying individual company stock in a mostly efficient market is a futile endeavor.

There are two types of risk in the stock market: systematic and non-systematic. (I know, I know. Exciting stuff, right? But don't skip this section just yet!) Every investment is vulnerable to *systematic risk*, like a massive earthquake or terrorist attack. There isn't much we can do about these events so we ignore them. *Non-systematic risk* is also called company-specific risk because it refers to the fact that any given company has its own set of business and operational risks. These include the risks of increased competition in their industry or an accounting scandal at their company.

The most important difference between the two types of risk is that non-systematic risk can be diversified away and systematic risk can't be. What this means to you is that if you own enough stocks, your portfolio will be somewhat padded from the problems of any individual company; that fire that broke out at one of their production plants isn't a big issue to you. One of the main reasons why an index tracking ETF is so appealing is that it allows you to diversify away non-systematic risk.

Most studies say that non-systematic risk can be mostly diversified away with roughly 30 stocks held in different industries. So why bother with ETFs, you ask? Well, an additional benefit of tracking large indexes is that they have a self-cleansing effect. Of the original 30 stocks included in the Dow Jones Industrial Average since inception in 1896, can you guess how many are still in business today? If you've guessed "one" then you are correct. (Ten extra points for knowing that it was General Electric.)

If you are surprised at the answer, this explanation might help. Of the original 30 stocks of the Dow Jones, 29 stocks failed and yet the Dow remains successful and has provided returns a thousand times over. How is that possible, you ask? Let's turn to Figure 13 of a standard bell curve:

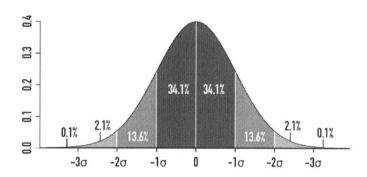

Figure 13: A bell curve.

On the right side of the bell curve are the indexes' top performers. As these companies are the biggest earners in a continually growing economy, only the sky is the limit as they return thousands of percent. On the left side, we have the weakest performers. The worst possible return from these companies can be negative 100% and bankruptcy. As the worst companies leave the index, such as the cotton and cattle companies of the original Dow, their positions are readily filled by new companies eager to take their place. This results in an upwards bias as the weakest companies leave the index and make room for newcomers, and the best companies are shifted to the right. You won't get this sort of self-correction, so to speak, in your own handpicked portfolio nor your advisor's fancy platinum-branded fund.

Maybe you've made some winning stock buys in the past couple of years and think you can keep it up. Before you do, make sure you look at your returns on a risk-adjusted basis! The *Sharpe ratio*, named after Nobel Laureate William Sharpe, gives us a way to examine the performance of an investment by adjusting for risk. For example, let's say that you invested in high-tech stock companies and speculative mining companies, and saw your money double in the past few weeks. There was a much higher chance that those companies could have gone bankrupt compared to your local utility provider or national telecom, and so you were rewarded proportionately to the level of risk that you took on. Similarly, there's a reason that your speculative Venezuelan Real Estate ETF pays an attractive dividend of 10%. The Sharpe ratio will tell you the price, in terms of extra volatility and uncertainty, which you pay for that extra return.

Sharpe was a smart man. In his 1975 study titled, *Likely Gains from Market Timing*[10] he concluded that for *market timers* (i.e. people making buy-or-sell decisions by attempting to predict future prices) to successfully beat the market, they must be accurate 74% of the time. Of course, these results don't take into account management fees or commissions. If you're paying an advisor 2% to time the market for you, they had better be right nearly every single time they decided to buy or sell!

So, what does all of this tell us? It tells us that it is time to give up trying to game the system. It's not worth the time or stress and you'll probably screw it up anyways. Rest easy, invest confidently with a passive index style, and focus your time on more meaningful matters. (Here's a hint: it's not money.)

Is there a stock investing strategy that you're interested in that we haven't touched on yet? Maybe you want to invest in companies with growing dividends

---

[10] http://www.jstor.org/stable/4477805

or safe companies like utility providers. I implore you to read the thorough Appendix B: The pitfalls of dividend investing.

Sleeping soundly: What if the ETFs fail? Or steal my money?

Sorry my friend, but nothing is risk-free in this world. Even if you hide your money under your mattress there is always the chance it catches on fire or rampant inflation devalues your currency to the extent that it's no better than kindling. Let's look at some of the safeguards in place to protect investors from ETF or brokerage failure.

When you buy any type of mutual fund, including exchange traded funds (ETFs), you own the underlying assets. If you buy $10,000 of a S&P 500 ETF and Apple is 2% of the S&P 500 then the ETF administrator holds $200 worth of Apple stock on your behalf. They can't move it, re-package it, nor re-sell it to someone else because it's yours. You have a right to that asset so even if the fund administrator goes bankrupt, they will distribute those Apple shares to you.

Vanguard, one of the more popular ETF administrators, is an interesting case study because they maintain a corporate structure established to protect individual investors. Instead of having an investment management company which owns and operates funds on behalf of clients, the funds themselves own the administrative company. In turn, the funds are owned by everyday investors in Vangaurd's ETFs, like you or me. This inverted structure means that were the management of Vanguard to go bankrupt, the funds could find a new suitor to run them.

Of course, you'll have to go through a brokerage to purchase ETFs in the first place. But online discount brokers are sometimes more user-friendly and almost always cheaper than brokerage arms of the big banks and credit unions. Many online brokerages even offer free ETF buys, meaning you won't ever have to let commissions bite into your returns.

Popular choices in Canada include *Questrade*[11], which has free ETF buys, *Virtual Brokers*[12], and *Qtrade*[13]. After creating an account at a brokerage and navigating to the buy/sell order form, you enter in the ticker symbol of any of the popular ETFs, including those from Vanguard[14] and iShares BlackRock[15].

In America, *TD Ameritrade*[16] is renowned for its customer service, but there are cheaper options like *Robinhood*[17], *Schwab*[18] and *E trade*[19]. Or, in America only, you can even hold an account directly with *Vanguard*[20].

There are even national safety nets. In the case of a brokerage failure in the United States, the *Securities Investors Protection Corporation* (SIPC) may step in to protect investors. The SIPC is a nonprofit industry membership organization that provides insurance to investors of up to $500,000. If your brokerage goes bankrupt, the first thing SIPC will do is offer to transfer your investments to another brokerage. If your brokerage, (in an attempt to not go bankrupt) was stealing and selling your investments, the SIPC will reimburse you up to a $500K limit. Many developed countries around the world have similar systems. The point is that you should sleep soundly. Investing on your own can make you richer *and* less stressed.

---

[11] http://www.questrade.com/
[12] https://www.virtualbrokers.com/en-us/
[13] https://www.qtrade.ca/
[14] https://www.vanguardcanada.ca/individual/etfs/etfs.htm
[15] https://www.blackrock.com/ca/individual/en-ca/products/product-list?nc=true&siteEntryPassthrough=true#!type=iSharesETFCA&tab=overview&view=list
[16] https://www.tdameritrade.com/home.page
[17] https://www.robinhood.com/
[18] https://www.schwab.com/
[19] https://us.etrade.com/home
[20] https://investor.vanguard.com/etf/

Chapter 4

Bonds, gold, and diversification

We talked a lot about stocks above but what about bonds, the other major part of the successful portfolios in the Trinity study? Unlike stocks, bonds don't represent a piece of a company; bonds are loans that a company or government owes to their holder. The benefit of being a debtholders is that they almost always have priority over shareholders in cases of bankruptcy so they are the first to recoup any losses. This makes bonds inherently less risky and as such they also give investors lower returns. In fact, bond returns from 2010 onwards have been extremely low; in some countries they produce less than 2%. This might lead you to some head scratching: if bond returns are so low, why even bother?

Most people know that bonds can make your portfolio less risky, but what exactly is risk anyway? Most often, risk is measured by volatility and is described as the stomach clenching ups and downs of a roller-coaster; the wild swings in a portfolio's value that makes it hard for us to sleep at night. If you need money in the next three months, you want to put it in something that is not volatile, like a savings account,. In the short-term at least, volatility is an excellent measure of risk.

Volatility is especially important in the withdrawal years of FI. Remember, the successful portfolios in the Trinity study gained about 7% a year on average but the concluded safe withdrawal rate (SWR) was only 4%. What is the reason for this difference between the two percentages? Well, it is salient to remember that the 7% was only an average. If your portfolio gained 7% each and every year, then that would also be its SWR. But there are many years when a portfolio which averages 7% might have losses of 20% or even more.

Withdrawing from your portfolio in one of those years with large negative returns in the beginning of the withdrawal stage can cripple your future positive returns. It takes a chunk out of your investments before they even have a chance to grow and compound. So losing a part of your *principal* right at the start of withdrawal can therefore increase your chance of portfolio failure significantly. This is not necessarily the case if you have a big negative loss *after* your portfolio has already experienced some positive gains for many years, because it's already had a chance to grow.

So how can we lower the risk that you'll wind up broke, dependent on government assistance or on the kindness of others after working so hard to achieve FI? It's here that I'm reminded of the popular phrase, "there's no such thing as a free lunch." This is always true, especially when it comes to investments, but for one exception and that is *diversification*.

Using the S&P 500 and US government bonds, Figure 14 demonstrates the relationship between risk and returns across 35 years. *Standard deviation*, as the square root of volatility, is a measure of risk shown on the horizontal axis and the average annual return is on the vertical axis.

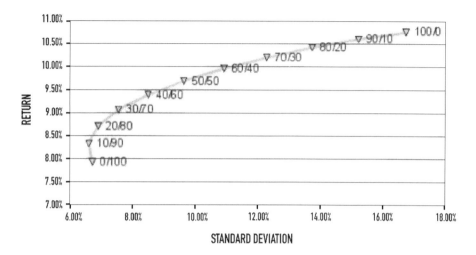

Figure 14: Expected return for a 1 year holding period.

Just like saving a little is better than nothing, this figure should give you the confidence to buy some bonds. Starting on the right side of Figure 14, we can clearly see that moving from a 100/0 to 90/10 allocation (or 100% stocks to 90% stocks) has a huge impact on volatility. Return, on the other hand, decreases by a relatively small amount. And after the halfway mark, as we move left, you can see that risk barely decreases as the returns become significantly smaller. There are diminishing returns (and reduced risk) on both sides of the graph.

Why is there such a big difference in volatility between a 100/0 stock-to-bond split and an 80/20 split? One of the reasons is a concept called *re-balancing*. Don't worry; this is not a complicated procedure. Re-balancing is accomplished by buying or selling assets (stocks or bonds) to return your portfolio to your desired allocation. For example, let's say that you are in the accumulation stage and your allocation goal is 70% equities and 30% bonds. On January 1st, your real life allocation may be similar to your goal but over time the valleys and hills of the stock market changes your allocation even if you didn't buy or sell anything. Halfway through the year, your portfolio might end up as 65/35, or 75/25, and you will have to sell or buy—thus re-balance your portfolio—to get back to your intended 70/30 split. In the accumulation phase, it might be easiest to rebalance simply by changing your buying habits. If your goal is a 70/30 split and stocks are currently 65% of your portfolio, you can simply make your next purchase stocks. We'll talk more about what the best allocation, i.e. the split between the investments in your portfolio, is for you, later.

A recurring theme on the quest to financial independence is how difficult it is for humans to make good long-term decisions. Throughout our evolution as a species, humans have cultivated an instinct of reacting to the here and now and that instinct can just easily manifest as the impulse to eat all of the food we can get our hands on before it spoils or selling after a stock market crash just to put it under the mattress. Everyone knows that in order to make money on the stock market you need to "buy low and sell high" but many struggle to actually execute that mantra.

The act of balancing your portfolio serves to take emotion out of buying and selling decisions and forces you to only sell high and buy low. This means that if equities made up 50% of your portfolio but your target was 60% then rebalancing would force you to sell what is relatively high (bonds) and buy what is relatively low (stocks) to get back to your initial goal of a 60/40 allocation. You've would have then lowered the average cost of your equities and increased gains in the future when they rise again. It also works the other way. Re-balancing would let you reduce portfolio risk by making sure you lock some gain in on your equities when they rise beyond your target and that you replace them with something less risky.

And it does work in real life. In 2005, the S&P 500 hit the 1,200 mark. The next time it hit this mark with upwards momentum was in 2010. To the untrained eye, it looks like investors must have been relieved to finally break even on their investment. This is true for people who didn't re-balance. Re-balancers in the withdrawal stage of FI were selling all the way up to the peak in 2007 and buying after the crash. They recovered months or years before people who didn't re-balance. Think of balancing your portfolio as timing the market except it's based on a consistent target instead of intuition.

A common concern of dividend investors is that they'll be forced to sell stocks at a loss. Their rationale is that by living off of their dividend income and never touching their principal, they'll never be forced to sell at a big loss. Wouldn't it have sucked to have been forced to sell some of your equities in order to pay your bills in 2008? With bonds, and re-balancing, you wouldn't have had to. Yes, stocks were down so far that people in the withdrawal stage of FI had to sell bonds in order to pay their bills and re-balance their portfolios but by the time they got back to their target allocation goal, those equities would've already started to increase in value again.

Designing a portfolio

So, what percentage of your portfolio should you allocate to bonds? The answer depends on your personal risk tolerance, which is your ability to stomach sharp drops in your investment account. However, perhaps even more than that, it depends on your time horizon. In the above section, we discussed how volatility is a good measurement of risk. But by definition volatility is a short-term phenomenon: it's the day to day or month to month swings in your portfolio. How can we measure portfolio risk in the long term?

The answer is that instead of looking just at the ups and downs of the rollercoaster ride, we need to look at the possible number of rollercoasters you could be on and the percentage of those that could end up on the moon or in at bottom of the Pacific Ocean. Mathematically, it is no longer enough to simply look at the short-term volatility of different portfolios; we need to look at the standard deviation of the distribution of returns. To do this, we'll need a new graph. The graph in the last section, Figure 14, only plotted one line for one year of returns. We'll need more lines that can show the results of longer holding periods.

The graph in Figure 15 doesn't use any historical data. Rather, it was made by me to illustrate the effects of a long holding period on long-term risk.

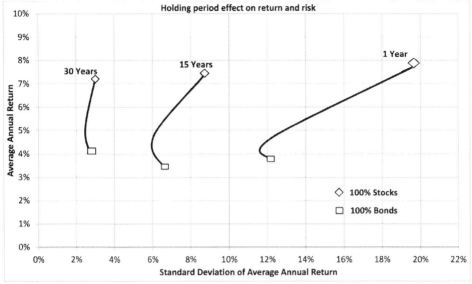

Figure 15: The impact of holding periods on risk and return. No historical data was used in the creation of this image; it's for illustrative purposes only.

As you can see, holding more bonds decreases the range of expected outcomes that are possible for a portfolio, but the effects of this diminish rapidly on a large enough time-scale. The more stocks you hold, the more likely it is that you are on a crazy rollercoaster that will lead you into the fiery depths of investment hell or to the promised land of yachts and vacation homes. But the longer you stay on that rollercoaster, the more likely it is that you will arrive safely at a reasonable destination.

This is the reason why you might hear people say things like "I'm young and have a high risk tolerance. I can handle volatility. Why wouldn't I hold 100% stocks?" If you have a time horizon of 30-years, then this approach can definitely make sense in the early years of accumulation. However, for many people trying to achieve FI in a shorter time frame, this isn't necessarily their best option. It's definitely not the least risky option available to them. The benefits of re-balancing are too great and the reduction of risk that can be achieved with a 90/10 portfolio or an 80/20 portfolio is too attractive for people with 10 or 20-year time horizons to ignore. And while most people should hold at least some bonds in the accumulation stage, the exact percentage will depend on your time horizon and personal preferences.

However, that's not to say that high outcome variance strategies are incompatible with *financial independence* (FI). One of the underlying themes of FI is flexibility and for some people taking risks can absolutely be a part of that. Imagine you are someone who has paid off their student loans and starts working a career at the age of 35. This person may have the goal of becoming FI by the age of 45, but they're willing to take risks to get their earlier. A 100% equity portfolio could mean that this person accomplishes their goals in 5 years, instead of 10. The downside is that it could instead also take 12 or 15 years. Some people thrive on this level of uncertainty and some others feel that their FI goals are non-negotiable; they've set a date and want to achieve it. But if you're willing to take the risk and be more flexible, you absolutely can justify a 100% equity portfolio.

Some people take this high outcome variance approach even further by advocating for *a small-cap tilt portfolio*. This strategy is based on holding more of the smaller companies because they have higher historical returns than bigger companies. The number of possible outcomes balloons with these kinds of approaches. Just like with 100% stocks, "I can handle the short-term volatility" is not a responsible justification for a small-cap tilt.

It's true. In the very long-run, we *can* expect small-caps to provide higher returns. How long is the very-long run? Well, the math involved here is beyond the scope of this book, but you can use the Sharpe ratio to calculate how many years you would need to hold small-caps for them to outperform other assets within certain confidence intervals. According to calculations done by Newfound Research, you would need to hold small-caps for about 120 years in order to be 95% confident that your return would be higher than the S&P 500.

The increased standard deviation of returns that comes with smaller companies isn't something most investors can handle. The majority of people seeking FI will want a target date within a couple of years and a small-cap tilt doesn't allow for this. A small-cap tilt is only defensible by people who are willing to be extremely flexible with their FI goals and target dates. That's not to say that you can't do it. By all means, go ahead. But make sure you understand the implications of this approach and are willing accept the consequences if things turn sour and you need to work for more years than you'd hoped. Alternatively, let's make plans now for you to send us postcards from Bermuda.

Bonds?! Are you crazy? Rates are going up!

We got a little sidetracked there with our discussion on the benefits of diversification. You're probably still wondering how bonds work and how you can get some. Okay, so let's look at a 5-year bond that is issued for $1,000 with a 6% coupon. That means you give the company or government (the issuer) $1,000, and they give you $60 every year, and they give your $1,000 back 5 years from now.

Now that's all fine and dandy but what happens if you want to sell the bond as part of re-balancing your portfolio or to pay your bills? Well, the price you can sell the bond for will depend on the going rates in the bond market. Imagine if after holding onto your bond for two years, the issuer was now selling bonds for $1,000 with a 12% coupon. Why would anyone want to buy your bond from you for $1,000, when they could go get one from the same issuer at a much higher coupon rate?

In order to sell your bond, you would have to lower its price. You might now only be able to sell it for $820. Of course, you don't have to. You can always just hang onto it and the issuer will give you the full $1,000 back at the end of the 5-year term. This is why it's important to think about how long you will be holding a bond for before you buy it, and to make sure the time to maturity (5 years in this example) is in line with your holding period.

But what about the person that buys your bond from you for $820? They're going to collect three more payments of $60 ($180) and the issuer will give them $180 ($1,000 - $820) more than what they paid for it. This brings their total return to be $360 ($180 + $180), or 44% before inflation ($360/$820) over 3 years and shows how higher interest rates result in higher yields.

In 2016, interest rates have been near all-time historic lows. If you buy a bond now, its value on the bond market could take a big hit if rates rise as they are expected to. Because of that, you'll need to make sure you're buying the right bonds that fit your expected investment time holding period. But you won't be buying individual bonds. Just like with equities, there are exchange traded funds (ETFs) that track big sections of the bond market. It's best to stick to these for diversification and select a bond ETF by looking at its *"duration"* to get a sense of the minimum time you'll need to hold the fund in order to not take a loss if rates rise.

Any price decline from rising interest rates will be offset by higher coupons on newly issued bonds in an aggregate bond fund. So, although the person in the above example may be dismayed by the drop in price of their bond to $820, they shouldn't fret if they hold it to maturity inside of an aggregate bond fund. In fact, they should be happy. The bond fund will buy some of those newly issued bonds with 12% interest rates, increasing the overall return of the bond fund in the future.

If you select an ETF that tracks an aggregate bond ETF, it'll try to track as many bonds as possible including both governmental and corporate bonds. For most people, this will be fine as a default option. One thing to stay away from is international bonds. Changes in foreign exchange rates complicate the returns used to help us predict what should be a reliable, low-risk part of your portfolio. If you're American and expect your future expenses once you've achieved FI to be in American dollars, there's no need to buy European or Canadian bonds. The same is true for Canadians.

Governments also issue lower risk products like *treasury bills (T-bills)* in the United States and *guaranteed investment certificates (GICs)* in Canada. These are secure shorter term investments, usually with a maturity of two years or less, and for that reason they don't have a big part to play in a long term portfolio. They are best used for situations like saving up for a down payment on a house or for school tuition that you'll spend in less than three years. If you insist on using them, make sure you have a low withdrawal rate. The returns on these investments are much lower than bonds and heavy use of them simply won't be able to support a 4% savings withdrawal rate.

In terms of actually buying bond ETFs, look no further than the most popular ETF providers in the market such as Vangaurd or iShares BlackRock in Canada, or Vanguard or Fidelity in America. Create an investment account at a brokerage, like we've already discussed, and enter your desired ETFs into the order form.

Gold's place in the modern portfolio: My precious (metals)

Some people have a fundamental anti-bond stance and they maintain this point of view even when shown the historical performance of bonds. This typically stems from mistrust in government, as most bonds in the market are issued by governments. So, I often get asked, can you use gold or another precious metal to balance your portfolio? The short answer is yes, but it's a bad idea.

The most important aspect of investments that you are going to re-balance is the strength of their inverse, or "negative," relationship. When interest rates go up, the coupon payment and yield on newly issued bonds also increase. Issuing bonds at higher rates means that it's more expensive for companies to borrow money, and as such they typically perform less well. Because of this, stocks and bond have historically had an inverse relationship.

As Figure 16 shows, the negative correlation of returns between stocks and bonds is crucial for re-balancing because it means you will be able to buy low and sell high. When stocks are at a high, you'll likely sell them to buy bonds which will likely not be at record setting high prices; and vice versa.

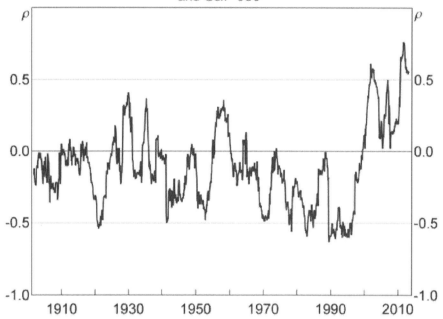

US Stock-Bond Correlations

Correlation of changes in 10-year government bond yields
and S&P 500*

* Three-year rolling centred correlation of monthly changes; Standard
  Statistics' 90 Stock Composite Index used prior to 1957
Sources: Global Financial Data; RBA

Figure 16: The correlation between stocks and bonds

With respect to precious metals like gold, their prices are also typically
negatively correlated with stock returns. When stocks take a big hit, some
investors flee to what is viewed as the safe haven of precious metals. But a
negative correlation isn't the only thing that we look for in an asset when re-
balancing our portfolio. It is also important that it actually provides some
returns. And as material object, gold fails to provide any returns. Notice how I
said the "price" of gold—not the return—is negatively correlated with stock
returns? That's because a hunk of metal in your dresser doesn't give you any
returns. It's not out there making any money for you. Bonds may not have a
perfect negative correlation, but at least they are actively doing *something* for
you while you wait to use them as a re-balancing tool.

Figure 17: Who says gold doesn't know what you want?

Is there a place for physical gold or metal in the modern diversified portfolio? Perhaps but it's a small one. You could always buy stocks of gold producing companies because, unlike physical gold, these companies actually seek to turn a profit and provide a return to you, but that would also add non-systematic risk to your portfolio and we've already been down that path. There's no need to take the gamble that gold mining companies will outperform the market on a risk-adjusted basis.

Furthermore, metal mining companies are already included in any total stock market index. Canadian investors may already be over exposed to the natural resource sector, including gold, as it makes up such a large part of the Canadian economy. Even holding an exchange traded fund (ETF) that includes every company in Canada isn't likely to give you much diversification because the economy as a whole isn't well diversified compared to the world at whole. This risk can be even further compounded if your job relies directly or indirectly on the price of a commodity. We'll discuss home country bias and foreign currency risk later when we talk about picking the right portfolio and in Appendix H: Is currency risk a part of a diversified portfolio?

Although, the Trinity Study was conducted using a stock and bond portfolio, it's interesting to see the historical returns and saving withdrawal rates (SWRs) of portfolios that include alternative asset classes. *www.portfoliocharts.com* maintains a fantastic visual guide to how portfolios such as the Golden Butterfly (which includes 20% gold holdings), and the Ivy Portfolio (which has been used by endowment funds at Harvard and Yale and includes 20% REIT holdings) have performed over long time periods. Spoiler alert: some have even out-performed a total stock and bond market approach but that doesn't necessarily make them the right choice for you. Historical gold returns are skewed by the metal's incredible performance in the 1970's. It's more likely that growth was a statistical anomaly than a repeatable achievement.

Chapter 5

Another way to FI: Your own business

Many people think that starting their own business will lead to riches. They may even see it as their only alternative to working at a job they don't like until they reach 65. The fruits of a successful business are definitely sweet and the pay-off can have bigger rewards than a job. Entrepreneurship isn't for everyone; for most people the potentially long delay to financial independence (FI) just doesn't make it worth the risk. If you're currently saving 3% of your income, you don't need to start a business to strike it rich; there's a good chance that you're sitting on a goldmine and your efforts are better focused on trying to find ways to stop spending it. A person who has no assets and can save 50% of their income can achieve FI in around 15 years. There is, however, a limit to how much spending you can cut. We'll talk more about how to increase your income, or choose a job, later.

Steady employment is the number one path the most people take to FI and it is that way for good reason. You get a paycheck every two weeks which means that it's easier to budget every month and project your time to FI with more certainty. You will probably also be less stressed compared to a business owner, allowing you to spend more time with your friends and family or doing things you love. There's nothing wrong with taking a sure path to FI instead of a potentially precarious one. Your personality will play a big role in your decision to become a business owner or not, so let's make sure the shoe fits.

If you do decide to lift yourself up by your bootstraps to enjoy the freedom that comes with being your own boss, make sure that your business is about something that you're passionate and knowledgeable. Sure, there are serial entrepreneurs who run around from one idea to the next but you're more likely to start a successful business when it's in an industry that you've been involved in and know the problems that need to be solved. When you're young, everyone tells you to take risks and try a business idea before you have a mortgage or kids to feed. This sounds like logical advice but a high percentage of these businesses will fail because the founders don't have the technical skills or networking contacts needed to succeed. Consider getting some experience under your belt during the day and starting your business idea on weekends.

Keep in mind that the advice to first get experience is entirely industry dependent. In some industries, like accounting or welding, it is impossible to go out on your own without some experience because of licensing and certification requirements. Other industries, like software engineering, are newer and have very few barriers to entry. Anyone with a passion for programming can create their own website or application and the industry shows it. People are leaving their mark on the software industry at a much younger age when compared to others. There's no one size fits all advice—you'll need to evaluate the industry that you're targeting and get a feeling of the value of employment experience.

Let's be clear that we are talking about *scalable businesses* here. A one-man plumbing shop or IT consulting gig may technically be a small business, but the work conditions are more similar to employment than CEO or president. If your business stops running the moment you walk out the door, then it's best to think of it as more like a job, albeit one with more freedom, because it relies on you completely to make sales. Being your own boss can be liberating and it is an especially interesting option for income supplement during the withdrawal years and we'll talk more about that later. For now, let's not confuse these options with a business that has employees and is capable of somewhat running itself after the start-up period.

To create a successful scalable business, you will need at least four things: expertise, dedication, a fitting personality, and luck. If you evaluate yourself and find you don't have all of the first three attributes, you should probably stay at your day job. When it comes to luck, you need to be in the right place at the right time. It is incredibly helpful to your potential success for your business to be in a growing industry. For example, think of telecom in the 90s, or e-sports and robotics now. Given the right environment (and luck) even some incredibly skilled people with bad leadership skills can make money in the right environment, and vice versa.

You know what else would be helpful? Hopefully you have a magician's hat from which you can pull out an unending supply of confidence and an ability to pick yourself up when you get knocked down. Wherever you look, the statistics on business failure rates are staggering. It's simply a very risky proposition for most people. And what is the trade-off for this risk? We know the opportunity cost of any money invested in starting a business is the 7% we would expect to earn from the stock-market in the long-run. For a small business to be worth the risk, you would typically expect a double-digit profit margin once it's past the start-up stage. That's because the true comparable isn't just the opportunity cost on the capital that you tie up in the business, but also needs to take into account the money you would earn at a full-time job working for somebody else as well.

Many small businesses do achieve that target of a double-digit profit margin. Knowing whether or not you'll achieve that level of profit is difficult, but being able to predict when you'll achieve it is even harder. This isn't a business projections course and you'll have to do a lot of research if you want to make predictions with any sort of accuracy. So, for many, the alternative is just to jump in and see if you float. If you're okay with losing some money, then this is a valid option. It also happens to be one of the reasons why so many businesses fail in the first place. Some serial entrepreneurs go through countless business concepts before one sticks. If you prefer that kind of lifestyle and you understand that this non-conventional route could delay your FI by many years, hop in and give your 110%.

110% - that's executive speak right there. You'll need to add some nonsensical motivational words to your vocabulary if you want to be a CEO. Try this on for size, "Okay team, we need to be proactive about developing some synergies in response to last month's ROI. Let's touch base with our partners to ensure we're evolving with the market and on pace to meet our leverage and core competency goals."

A lot of successful businesses are started by people who are already on their way to financial independence and have some sort of security buffer. Undoubtedly, there will be some lean months in any new business, and you will want to avoid taking a salary at first so you can re-invest profits back into the operations. If it's at all possible, you should continue working your day job as long as possible and start by building your business in your free time. At the very least, consider waiting until you have some type of financial security so that you're not worried about putting food on the table and delivering a product at the same time.

If you are not sure about your comfort level with starting a business, you could always wait until you are FI and start it then. There are many people who are truly passionate about something but are risk-averse and this is the best option for them.

Figure 18: Founder, Director, CEO, and President of To Be Determined Inc. Have a passion for something other than being in charge and having a big ego.

Side hustles and moonlight income

Whether you're on the sure path of a professional career or the steady march of employment, you may get antsy and crave some more income. Without going back to school to learn gain new skills or changing industries, there are many opportunities for you to speed up your timeline to financial independence (FI). There are always avenues to get some extra cash by walking dogs, babysitting, or delivering newspapers. With the rise of the sharing economy and technology, it's easier than ever to moonlight as an Uber driver or even make impressive amounts of passive income from YouTube or blogging ventures.

These opportunities are usually in areas that will become self-evident to you because they're things that you're passionate about. If you love wood working and you can make money from posting video tutorials or by selling your creations online, then do it. That's fantastic. You're making money and enjoying yourself at the same time! What you need to avoid is side hustles that aren't particularly enjoyable for you. If you, for example, run early in the morning and would like the mindless peacefulness of running a paper route before their 9-5, then do it. But be wary if it sounds like a grind.

Don't let the desire to achieve FI overwhelm you. Remember that the goal of FI isn't just to save up a lot of money and live off of passive income. The goal is ultimately to allow you to focus on the things that truly matter by removing money worries and giving you free time. If your side hustle is stressing you out, or you're working eighty hour weeks just so you can achieve FI, then you're doing it wrong. Achieving FI won't even make you happy if you are miserable while you're working towards it. Think of Christmas as a kid or your high school graduation: sure there's a lot of anticipation leading up to the milestone but once you graduate or retire you're still you and the world moves on. Plan for the future but don't forget that enjoying the present is an important part of maximizing your happiness.

Chapter 6

Real estate: I need something more real!

Throughout history, whether it's been on American cotton plantations, English manors, or collective farms in the Soviet Union, land ownership has had a strong correlation with wealth. So it's no surprise that people from varying cultures have a fascination, or even an obsession, with real estate. Grandchildren around the world have had it instilled into them from a young age that owning property is the key to prosperity. But are our elders correct? Does this supposedly infallible wisdom hold up over time? And how does modern real estate compare to historical land and farm ownership?

What is real estate anyways? In the 21st century, housing is a commodity. Similar to precious metals and oil, when the demand for housing goes up, housing prices will follow and rise. If there is a boom of condo construction in your area, the price of your home could fall due to an over-supply of roofs to cover people's heads. Investment in property differs from an equity investment because the intrinsic purpose of a house isn't to make money, it's to provide shelter. Unlike a stock, homeowners can't hold anyone accountable when their profits aren't in-line with their budgets and expectations. And unlike landowners of past, homeowners don't have any peasants to threaten if the profitability of their real estate isn't up to snuff.

Of course, real estate *can* be a business; it's just not necessarily its natural state. A cursory look at the Toronto stock exchange shows that *Real Estate Income Trusts* (REITs) make up nearly 5 percent of the index's market cap, or total dollar value. Real estate transactions also account for more than 15% of economic activity in Canada as measured by *gross domestic product* (GDP). How does such a significant aspect of our world factor into your path to financial independence?

Rent vs. Buy: Real estate as a place to live

Let's think about real estate in two different ways: as an investment vehicle and as a home. First, you're going to have to live somewhere. And isn't rent just "paying someone else's mortgage"? The truth is not quite that simple. Both owning and renting have their place at some point in most people's lives. Real estate transactions will likely be the largest financial decisions that you are ever a part of, so you want to make sure you get it right. How does owning a home fit into the 4% safe withdrawal rate (SWR) concluded on by the Trinity study?

Your personal living space does not generate any passive income for you. This means that you don't get to add the value of your house to your stocks and bonds when calculating your SWR. However, owning a house *could* lower your annual expenses, and therefore your FI number as well, causing you to need less money to be financially independent. For this reason, we're not going to think about buying a house to live in as 'an investment', per se, even though it is such a big part of your financial life. It's hard to predict capital appreciation of real property, and growth in the value of your home is not something you should be banking on for your retirement. Instead, in the context of financial independence, it's better to think of your housing needs as part of your ongoing expenses.

There is a simple rule of thumb in the perpetual 'rent vs. buy' battle royale: if you're going to stay in a place for less than 5 years, always rent. If you're going to stay in a place for more than 10 years, always buy. Are you staying in-between 5 and 10 years? Well, it can get complicated. When in doubt, rent.

There are two main reasons why this rule holds true. The first is closing costs. Usually sellers pay commissions of around 6%, which comes from the cash they get from selling their house, to their agent, who splits that 50/50 with the buyer's agent. Add on to that land transfer taxes for 1 or 2%, moving costs, and legal fees, and it's easy to see how these expenses can add up to nearly half of your down payment. Even though these expenses come out of your pocket in the year you move into a new property, you can conceptually average them out over the number of years you live in that location. By staying in one house for as long as possible, you decrease the cost per year of these one-time expenses.

The second reason is interest. The way a mortgage works is that when you make a payment on it, a portion goes to the principal of the loan, which becomes your home equity, and a portion is interest, I.e. a fee paid for borrowing money that you'll never get to see again. The interest, the part that is a non-recoverable expense, will always be higher at the beginning of the loan, especially during the first 5 years.

We can illustrate this with math on a condo is Mississauga. Let's imagine a $100,000 loan with monthly payments of $422, and an interest rate of 3% per year on a 30-year mortgage. When the first payment is made on this mortgage, the interest portion is the monthly interest rate [3% divided by 12] X $100,000 = $250. The portion of the $422 payment that is not interest [$422-$250 = $172] goes towards the $100,000 debt, reducing the amount you owe to the bank and therefore also reducing future interest payments.

When you make a payment of $422 in the 20th year of this mortgage, the portion that relates to interest will be much lower. By then, the remaining loan will be down to $40,000 and the monthly interest is calculated as [3% divided by 12] X $40,000 = only $100, down from $250 in the first year. Simply put, the percent of a mortgage payment that is "paying yourself", increases with every payment you make. It is truly in the later stages of a mortgage that the principal can be paid down quickly, building your home equity.

For the two following reasons, selling a house within the first 5 years of a mortgage is almost always a bad move: you'll pay a ton of fees and won't have much equity to show for your monthly payments. Let's analyze the same Mississauga condo from a 'rent vs. buy' perspective. To do this, we need to make up a detailed comparison by adding up all the costs for renting a property versus owning a property, over the time that you expect to live there. We need to take into account the opportunity cost of your down payment, which is the 7% or so that you could expect to earn if you rent and invest that down payment into the stock market. We also need to estimate the rent increases per year (say 2% per year, the maximum increase in many jurisdictions), the growth of the home's market value (say 4% per year, including 2% inflation), and the interest rate of the mortgage over the time you'll live there.

But there's no need to re-invent the wheel here. There is an abundance of 'rent vs. buy' calculators available online, the most notable of which is from the *New York Times*[21]. Canadians should keep in mind that your marginal tax rate isn't applicable, as property tax and mortgage interest isn't deductible in Canada, so you can go ahead and bring that down to zero. The calculator works by finding the total costs of ownership for the property that you've entered and giving you the break-even rent amount. This is the amount at which renting the property would cost the same as buying it. If you can rent it for less than that amount, you should rent, and vice-versa. I input the assumptions we made about the Mississauga condo above into the New York Times calculator for a 10 year stay and the break-even point for rent was roughly $1,700 per month.

Here's another rule of thumb: condos are costly. Condos can be great for quality of life but don't expect that buying one will be a beneficial financial move. The condo board maintenance fees can really add up, so you'll need a ton—more than our estimated 4% per year—of growth in the value of the condo for it to be worth it. The Mississauga condo in question can be rented for $1,300 a month, meaning that owning it is about $400 more expensive per month than renting it; $48,000 more over 10 years.

Buying can also tie you down to a geographical location and may make it more difficult for you to take a job that increases your earnings power. It's hard to overstate how valuable mobility can be and renting grants you that flexibility. So, think about your future work prospects and job stability when making a decision. If you might be changing employers every couple of years, then it

---

[21] http://www.nytimes.com/interactive/2014/upshot/buy-rent-calculator.html?_r=0

could make a lot of sense to rent and re-locate closer to your new workplace every few years. You'd even be able to cut down on commuting time and costs which would allow you to save even more.

Figure 19: A quick move

Psychologically, people often prefer to own a house because it feels more secure, like it is theirs and nobody else's. They can do what they please and no-one can kick them out! Of course, we know that's not true. If you can't pay your property tax, water, or mortgage bills, you will eventually get evicted. Having a hoard of investment money and living in a rental is just as much of a security measure as owning your own home.

A common, but ultimately indefensible, justification for buying is that a mortgage can act as retirement savings. Having equity in a house is great but paying tens to hundreds of thousands of dollars in interest to a bank for the privilege of being allowed to use your house like a piggy bank is a poor pretense that usually signals larger problems. If you have enough money to pay a mortgage but not enough to rent while putting away money for investments, you need to go back and re-visit the 'rent vs. buy' calculator or take control of your frivolous spending. Paying your mortgage and living paycheck to paycheck every month is easy but financial independence (FI) is about doing what makes sense rather than what's easy.

Of course, there could be many reasons why owning a place might be the right decision for you, even if it isn't the best financial decision to make. Owning real estate can be a real source of personal pride. And there are some things you just can't do in a rental. Perhaps you want the freedom to renovate or landscape. Maybe you want a stable environment for your children with the guarantee that they'll be able to stay at one school for their entire childhood. Or perhaps you're willing to work a couple of extra years if it means being able to live close to your friends and family. It's better to be happy and working than retired and miserable.

There are many places in the country where buying is the right financial decision. Even if it's not, you can still justify it. Just make sure that you understand the impact that it will have on your FI.

What to look out for when buying real estate

If the numbers make sense, or you're simply set on buying, there are a few crucial things to take into consideration before you buy. Above we talked about how the seller always pays commission to real estate agents out of the proceeds on the sale of the house. A typical split would be 3% each to the seller's agent and the buyer's agent. So as the buyer, even though it may feel like you aren't paying commission because you aren't writing a check, you actually are paying. It's just done indirectly through the seller.

Does anything seem peculiar about that set-up? If you smell something funny, your intuition might just be right. Like the mutual fund and financial advisor industry, the real estate industry is an entrenched, archaic model that hasn't changed in decades.

As a home buyer, you expect your real estate agent to barter on your behalf for the lowest possible price on a home. But what incentive do they have to do that, when their commission comes out of the proceeds of the sale? The more you pay for a house, the more your real estate agent gets paid! The agent may act like they're on your team but their incentives aren't necessarily set-up that way.

Of course, real estate agents still have the incentive of gaining satisfied customers and that's what all agents aim for. Their biggest pay-off is parlaying your positive experience into recommendations and access to your friends, and they aren't likely to get that unless they deliver at least a reasonable price on a home.

Buying a house for $400,000 instead of $380,000 gives the buying agent only $600 more, which is hardly worth it compared to the increased business that satisfied customers can bring.Is your real estate agent really going to want you to pay more for a house when it translates into so little compensation for them? That seems unlikely. But wait—isn't the same also true for the selling agent? Why would a seller agent hold out for an offer of $20K more when it would only benefit them an additional $600? Wouldn't their efforts be rewarded more if their client took the $380,000 offer, so that they could move on to the next sale?

Real estate agents can be lovely, talented, and helpful people that may even go out of their way to help you either sell your house for the highest price possible or find exactly what you're looking for. But it's an understatement to say that their incentives aren't aligned with your best interests. Real estate agents make money by closing on a large volume of transactions. An extra $10,000 on a sale price of a home may be a lot of money to you but it only represents $300 to your agent. That's why there is so much pressure to accept deals and wrap things up.

So, what's the solution to an industry with built-in misaligned incentives at best and predatory practices at worst? Well, you can always keep renting. Without being entirely 'tongue in cheek', renting is a viable option. And if you're intent on buying, consider doing it yourself (DIY). DIY is a common theme in financial independence. If you're looking at a standard cookie-cutter home in a suburb, an agent will provide very limited value. Do a lot of research and look up comparable sales of similar homes in the neighbourhood. Know your limit and don't be intimidated by other agents. Oh, and don't be afraid to spend money on a lawyer and home inspector. They'll save you more money than a realtor.

Real estate agents can still provide good value and service for homes that are unique or of high value. At the very least, you'll have access to the agent's dedicated network of motivated buyers and sellers. Just remember where your agent's incentives lie. If you insist on using one, consider asking them to work on an hourly basis. Many will agree to this and you still get their services without their bias. Just like DIY investing, DIY home buying is increasingly common as young people re-evaluate the traditional ways of doing things.

Should I pay off my mortgage or buy investments?

Let's say after all your bills are paid for the month, you're left with some extra cash. Should you use it to pay off your mortgage, leaving you debt free earlier? Or should you buy some low-fee exchange traded funds (ETFs)? The answer is not always straightforward, with each option having both pros and cons, and it depends largely on your personal risk tolerance.

Paying down your mortgage means that you'll save on interest costs in the future. Think of this as a guaranteed return on investment. Wow, a guaranteed return! That sounds like a pretty good deal and it is good. But the alternative, investing in equities, could provide even greater returns. If you have a recent mortgage, it is likely at a less than 4% interest rate. Compared to historical equity returns, your mortgage might actually be giving you a pretty paltry return. Of course, that is just in the long run. If your risk tolerance can stomach short-term losses, then consider buying the equities.

Now, the above doesn't mean that you should avoid paying off your mortgage or other debt in favour of buying investments. Debt is a funny thing and people often feel constrained by it even if they have the means to pay it off but choose not to. If having debt keeps you up at night, then why subject yourself to that stress? It may not make pure financial sense but there's a point where your personal well-being might trump your spreadsheets and formulas.

Sometimes it can be helpful to push logic to extreme scenarios to see if it still holds up. Let's say you owe a million dollars on your mortgage and tomorrow you win the lottery for a million dollars. Congratulations! You should put it all into investments, in order to maximize your returns, right? Well, what would you do if the situation was reversed? Imagine you owned a paid off house worth a million dollars. Would you borrow a million dollars against your home in order to invest in the stock market?

For most people, the answer is likely no. Even though logically and mathematically the two scenarios are equivalent, the psychological comfort of that guaranteed return can't be overstated. Very few investments have no variance, and that fact has an added emotional value to the pay-off scenario when compared to the various outcomes possible with other investments. There's no easy answer here. But when you figure out what percentage of those million dollars that you would be willing put into your investment accounts, then you've found your risk tolerance.

Let's put this another way: taking out a mortgage instead of buying a house with cash means that your net worth will likely be higher at the end of the mortgage. That's because your investment portfolio will provide higher returns than the house over that time period. However, this approach will also lead to a lower portfolio success rate. You'll be slightly more likely to run out of money because your annual expenses will be higher with a mortgage than with a cash purchase. High expenses during market downturns can be devastating to portfolio success rates because you'll still have to pay your mortgage when your stocks take a hit. (We discuss how to improve on these scenarios in the next chapter, Critiquing and learning from the Trinity Study.

Americans have more incentive than Canadians to keep their mortgage around while also investing in equities because mortgage interest is tax deductible in the "Land of the Free." This means that the guaranteed return from paying off a mortgage might be lower in the United States than in Canada.

Having extra money to pay towards your mortgage or investments each month is a good problem to have. It means you're not spending your entire paycheck and are on your way to financial independence! No matter what decision you make, you will see some sort of return. It's a win-win scenario so don't let it stress you out too much.

Digital nomads and geographic arbitrage

What makes sense in one real estate market may not make sense in another. The extreme local nature of the real estate market demonstrates how distinct different economies around the world can be. Desirable places to live generally have higher costs for items ranging from groceries to car repairs. In order to attract people to these high cost of living (COL) areas, employers have to factor this into their employees' pay.

For example, let's look at software engineer Steven who lives in the mid-west United States which is a relatively low COL area. Steven currently makes $70,000 a year after taxes. His rent is only $500 a month and he buys a lot of cheap food straight from the nearby farms. By living frugally and only buying what he needs, Steven is able to save half of his salary or $35,000 a year. As his annual spending is also $35,000, Steven's financial independence (FI) number is $875,000.

Based on his current savings rate, Steven can expect to achieve FI in about 15 years. But what if he moved to a high COL place like Silicon Valley? There, he could command a bigger salary, $200,000. In order to maintain his 50% savings rate, Steven could live with roommates and limit his taste for all of the expensive new restaurants that aren't as plentiful back home. It might feel like a significant sacrifice but it is possible. And if he is able to save $100,000 a year in Silicon Valley, he would be able to achieve his goal of $875,000 much faster. In about 6 or 7 years, he would be able to head back to the mid-west with enough money to enjoy life and never work again.

Now that is an extreme example but it illustrates the main principles of geographic *arbitrage*. It doesn't work for everyone. I can already hear the disdain from small towners at the suggestion of moving to a alienating big city to get ahead. On the other side are city lovers who are asking themselves if life would even be worth living if they had to spend it more than a mile from the nearest artisan coffee shop. It is important that both groups understand the implications of their decisions; a little bit of flexibility can go a long way on the journey to FI.

Similar to the above example is the classic case of people retiring to different, usually tropical, countries like Costa Rica or Thailand. This can be a fantastic way for people to lower their expenses but you also have to be comfortable with the life offered in these countries as full-time residents, not tourists. Important services like healthcare and transit operate incredibly differently, and living so far away from your home country means you might not make it back for every holiday. It may seem like common sense but it is a life changing commitment; make sure to spend an extended amount of time in the area you are thinking of moving to before committing.

What if Steven was able to keep his Silicon Valley salary while working remotely from a beach in the Philippines? Digital nomads are people that are able to take geographic arbitrage a step further and earn western salaries while travelling the world or living in a very low COL place. A quick internet search of the term "digital nomad" will bring you to the experiences and strategies of people making this approach work for them. These types of lifestyles can be extreme for you both in the cultural sense and financial sense. Now, I'm not telling you to go out learn computer programming or to live out of a back-pack in Belize, but do take geographic arbitrage into consideration of your FI plans if it sounds appealing.

Another way to FI: Real estate as an investment

Residential and commercial real estate as an asset class is incredibly risky. Don't let anyone tell you otherwise. Remember that non-systematic risk that we talked about in regards to stocks above? Recall our conclusion that non-systematic risk can be virtually eliminated through diversification, or by holding at least 30 different stocks. Guess what—owners of rental properties can diversify risk away. An influx of condo construction in your geographic area, job loss in your area, or the raising of interest rates by central bankers are all risks that affect your investment returns. Even things on a smaller scale could impact you: your neighbours could cut down those scenic trees, or the quality of schools in your area could drop. If you decide to invest in single family homes or apartment buildings because stocks are too risky for you, you need to re-evaluate your rationale.

And if you're taking on debt to score those rental properties, your investment profits or losses will be magnified. Mortgage debt is the single largest source of leverage for individuals. Try going into a bank and asking for a million-dollar loan to put into an index tracking exchange traded fund (ETF) with a straight face. It's just not going to happen. It's ironic because unlike equity markets, which represent a large portion of our species' quantifiable productivity, there is no rule or evidence that commodities (such as local housing) must go up over time. Let's examine how leverage magnifies both profits and losses in a simplified example for illustrative purposes.

Graeme puts $100,000 down on a $500,000 duplex and dutifully pays the mortgage for 5 years. After 5 years and $50,000 in principal payments, he owes the bank $350,000 and his house is now worth $600,000. After selling it, and paying off the bank loan, Graeme is left with $250,000, of which $100,000 is profit [$250,000 - $100,000 - $50,000 = $100,000]. So, how great is Graeme's return? A $100,000 profit on a $500,000 home represents a 20% total return. At first glance, that may seem like an amazing return but remember that it took 5 years. If we take a simple average, the return becomes 4% a year and considerably less than the S&P 500 historical average.

However, there is more to this story! Graeme used leverage, which means that his $100,000 profit wasn't made on a $500,000 property. In fact, it was made with only a $100,000 down payment, meaning he is up 100%! That's right, he doubled his money in 5 years, or if we take a simple average, that's a 20% yearly return. Amazing, right?

Let's see what happens when the pendulum swings the other way.

What if, after 5 years, Graeme's property had decreased in value by $100,000? He still owes the bank $350,000 but now his house is only worth $400,000. Now, let's suppose that after a job loss and tenant vacancies, he has to sell his house at less than what it's worth. If he's lucky, he'll be able to pay the bank back at least what he owes them, $350,000, after selling the house. But if the property ends up worth less than $350,000, he would be holding what's called an *underwater mortgage* because he holds negative home equity. Needless to say, that would not be a good situation. His loss of $100,000 on a $500,000 property equals -20% in total, or -4% a year. But when we account for his leverage, he actually lost 20% a year, or 100% of his down payment. If the price of the property was less than $350,000, his return would've been worse than 100% because he would have lost more than his down payment; after the sale of his house, he would owe the bank more money.

This is the very real risk of being a small-time landlord who is restricted to one geographical area. Genuine diversification in real estate for a single investment property would be a house with a kitchen in San Jose and a bathroom in Boston—it's just not possible! And leverage will either light your returns on fire or you could end up wishing that you could light your house on fire to collect the insurance money. Tread carefully.

Why is real estate so popular if it is incredibly risky? Well, with great risk comes great potential returns, and with great returns come money that could singlehandedly shave years off the time it takes to reach financial independence (FI). Let's look at Oksana who needs $1,400 in passive income each month ($16,800 / yr.) to be financially independent. She has two options:

(1) Invest in equities and bonds. (Using a 4% savings withdrawal rate (SWR), she would need $420,000 invested.) Or,

(2) Purchase four properties that net her $350 per month each. In her area, these properties cost $300,000 each, and she would be required to put a down payment of $45,000 on each one. She would achieve financial independence with only $180,000 in down payments.

Wow, the second option requires $240,000 less! She could potentially shave years off of her required working life and ride freely into the sunset! Oksana could even re-finance after 5 or 10 years and expand to buy even more properties thereby increasing her passive income. Of course, managing real estate can be a lot work which doesn't exactly qualify as passive. Dealing with tenants is a hassle, especially if you're otherwise retired and just want to relax. And what if the government introduces new rent control laws? Or interest rates increase to 15 or 20%, like both Canada and the US experienced in the 1980s? Those kinds of rates would drive up her mortgages and obliterate her cash flow!

Nonetheless, the potential is there for real estate to provide astronomical progress on the road to financial independence. It would be in remiss to ignore how it worked out historically well for some normal, middle class workers who used real estate to make themselves into millionaires.

So, the gains can be great even though the risks can be even higher. And if you're going to take on this huge level of risk, you'd better ensure that you are compensated well for it. Let's take a look at how to properly evaluate a potential real estate investment. The real estate community has some common rules and ratios that they use to quickly calculate if a property is worthy of further consideration. This is very superficial analysis but comparing properties at this high level can give you an idea of where to focus.

Monthly rent to purchase price ratio: the higher this ratio is, the better. Did you find a place that costs $250,000 to buy and rents out for $2000/month? The rent to purchase price ratio is .008 or just less than 1%. To compare, the gold standard for this ratio used to be 2% but the number of geographic areas that meet 2% is getting smaller and smaller.

The 50% rule: if you hold a property for the long term, expect your expenses to be equal to a minimum of 50% of your rental income. This is a great rule to estimate the profitability of potential investments but is no excuse for not using real or more detailed data when you have it.

The 70% rule: this rule helps calculate the maximum you should pay for a house that needs rehabbing, i.e. extensive repairs and maintenance, before you flip it. Work backwards by estimating what the house will be worth after your renovations, and then multiply that by 70%. Then subtract the cost of the repairs and you arrive at an amount that will make this flip worth your time. Compare that figure to the list price to see if you should pursue the opportunity further. Flipping a house is a lot of work and FI is about the pursuit of mostly passive income.

After you've targeted a couple of properties with the rules above, it's time to delve into deeper analysis. In the real estate game, cash flow is king. If your properties aren't giving you money each month, they will slowly bleed you out. To evaluate cash flows, you need to add up all of our expected cash inflows and deduct our expected cash outflows. Sounds easy, right? But this simple exercise is the primary factor that most failed real estate investors screw up.

The best way to make an educated estimate is through experience. If you're trying to get a handle on what electricity might cost in one area, or the value of a parking spot, don't simply guess; get up and ask people first-hand. If you've never lived in an area before, you can't do too much research. Talk to realtors, contractors, or other local investors. Better yet, call up a property management company and ask how their vacancy rates in one city compare to another. Average utility costs could be made available by your province or state. Check out Kijiji or Craigslist and graph average rent prices in your area over time. It will take a lot of time and research which is also by no means a passive activity. And if the opportunity is right, jump in. You'll learn most by doing.

It's almost human nature to be bad at making accurate estimates, a problem that is seemingly compounded when money is involved. This makes it very difficult for investors to make an accurate analysis of their proposed investments. So be honest with yourself and, when in doubt, pick the conservative option.

To see real-world analysis of an investment property, see one of my first blog posts at www.graemefalco.com. You should also be sure to check out some of the investment property calculators online, like this one at *Good Mortgage*[22].

---

[22] http://www.goodmortgage.com/Calculators/Investment_Property.html

Chapter 7

Critiquing and learning from the Trinity Study

When the Trinity Study was developed in the 1990s, its creators wanted to hamper expectations for people who had ridden the big bull market up and thought they could use a 10-15% savings withdrawal rate (SWR). After the massive stock returns of the 90s, a 4% SWR looked paltry. Now, after a prolonged recession and slow economic take-off, people are naturally inferring from recent trends that even a 4% SWR might be too high. The truth is likely somewhere in the middle but to understand if that's the case, we need to return to the Trinity study and examine some of the assumptions upon which it was based.

One of the main criticisms of the Trinity Study is the rigidity of its spending model: whereby people would withdraw 4% of the initial portfolio balance every year, adjusted only for inflation. In real life, people will likely have some flexibility to their spending habits. *http://www.cfiresim.com* allows you to model historical simulations with various different spending plans, including one with a max spend during portfolio upswings and a minimum spend during downturns. Even a bit of flexibility like moving from 4% of initial portfolio value to 3% during a stock market crash can have dramatic effects on portfolio success rates. Play with the calculator yourself and you'll find ways to increase portfolio success rates from the 95% shown by the Trinity Study.

The Trinity Study also assumes that once you start withdrawing from your FI stash, you'll never work another day in your life. Just like decreasing your expenses, finding some part-time work during a stock downturn means you won't have to worry about selling parts of your portfolio at a bad time. Of course, finding a job or other source of revenue during a recession is easier said than done. But it doesn't have to be a large income to make a difference. Even tutoring for a couple of hours a week or doing seasonal work can vastly increase the chances of portfolio success.

Not only does the Trinity Study assume that you won't work after FI, it also assumes you'll never get any government assistance in the future. Now I won't get into the stability and solvency of Social Security in the United States or Old Age Security in Canada, but it's worth mentioning that The Canada Pension Plan is very robust and Canadians should absolutely expect to see benefits from it. For the sake of conservative estimates, a lot of people prefer to exclude government income in their projections to see if they can handle not getting any benefits. This is fine – but in reality, it's safe to say that most people in the western world should expect to receive *something* from their government to help them in old age. *http://www.cfiresim.com* allows you to model some income from government sources as well, so don't forget to take include them in your simulations! Poke around on some government websites to determine what a conservative estimate would be.

Another major criticism of the Trinity Study is that it only looked at 30 year periods and that for early retirees, this short time period is almost useless. While it is true that some people may want a withdrawal stage longer than 30 years, the biggest risk factor for portfolio failure is the sequence of returns. This means that the portfolios most likely to fail are ones that entered the withdrawal stage right before a market downturn, leading to people having to sell investments at a loss and their portfolios never recovering. There is a big difference in risk for people who started withdrawing 4% in 2007 compared to people who started withdrawing halfway through 2009. For this reason, almost any portfolio that is still going strong at 30 years will still be there at 40 or 50.

You can run longer simulations of the website I linked above but you'll start to run into the problem of not having enough data to draw meaningful conclusions as there is less than 150 years of useful stock market data on which to run historical simulations.

Making predictions about how long you'll need your stash for is one of the hardest parts of choosing a FI number. What if the average lifespan extends and you live to be 120 years old? Predicting the length of your life and the cost of old-age healthcare can be just as difficult as predicting the future value of your portfolio. All we can do is guess but it's good to take a conservative approach, as no-one wants to be 90 years old and unable to afford the quality of care they need to live comfortably. But beware of the "golden handcuffs", or "one-more year syndrome". Too many people continue working past FI at jobs they don't like because they want a super low withdrawal rate, just to be sure. What good is that extra comfort at 90 if they're not truly living now?

One portfolio strategy to reduce *sequence of returns risk*, i.e. the effects of retiring right before a recession, is to use a different asset allocation than the one used in the Trinity Study. Research by Wade Pfau PhD, found that a "glide path" to higher equity allocations protected a portfolio during its most vulnerable years. For example, instead of starting off the withdrawal stage with 40% bonds as tested in the Trinity Study, a retiree might start off with 70% bonds and slowly work down to 40% or 30%. Buying more stocks might be a hard or emotional sell to people who have already been comfortably retired for some years but it's an interesting option.

Richard's retirement was everything he ever dreamed of...

...for the first minute.

Figure 20: Financial crisis: sequence of returns risk.

Another option overlooked by the rigidity of the Trinity Study is semi-retirement. For example, let's take someone who needs $40,000 per year in retirement and therefore has a FI goal of one million dollars. After working for 10 years and investing $35,000 per year, this person will hopefully up with around $500,000. Assuming a 7% real return and the same $35,000 per year savings, they'll need to work another 6 years or so to reach their FI goal. Another option is to just leave that stash alone and let it grow. Left alone, that $500,000 stash will grow to be a million dollars in just over 10 years. If this person can pick up enough supplementary income—perhaps teaching as a lecturer for 4 months in the year, working a seasonal job, or continuing at their old job for 2 or 3 days a week—to cover their expenses for 10 years without dipping into their 500K stash, semi-retirement is very feasible.

Chapter 8

Projections, budgets, and the big three expenses

One complaint people have with projections is that it's so difficult to predict what their expenses will be in the future. And it's true, when most people start planning for financial independence (FI) they have no idea when they will want to retire or even what city they will want to live in. For this reason, it's a folly for young people to even have a firm FI number as there are still so many major life choices for them to make. Where they want to live, if they'll marry, have kids, or fund those kids' educations can all change your future expenses and it's impossible for young people to know the answer to all of these questions. Deciding on a particular FI number at the beginning of the FI journey isn't realistic or even helpful. For most people, it's best to simply save and invest as much as you can and worry about a firm number later, once those big decisions have been made. You don't know what your future self will want to spend money on but you can give your future-self more options.

What will your expenses actually be in retirement? There's a valid rationale for your expenses to decrease in retirement: you won't have to drive to work, buy fancy work clothes, and you could even find time to do more maintenance around the house instead of hiring it out. Of course, some people have their expenses go *up* during retirement because of international travel and more time for swanky golf memberships. It's all up to you.

The traditional advice found in the financial magazines that littered your doctor's office was to expect to your expenses to be 70% of what your pay checks were once you retire. Keep in mind that this was a supposed to be a one size fits all approach for the average American family that consumes like crazy. If you're on the path to FI and want to retire before 65, this generic advice won't be particularly useful to you. No book or magazine can tell you how much you'll spend in the withdrawal stage. You'll want something more personalized. Once you get comfortable creating a budget and give some good thought to the types of activities you plan to do in the withdrawal stage, you'll be able to give yourself a good extrapolation from your current expenses.

One thing that that is absolutely worth doing, no matter where you are on the path to FI, is creating a budget. But to budget for the future, you first need to have information from the past. Record your spending each month in a simple spreadsheet or using a budgeting tool like You Need a Budget (*YNAB*[23]). Laying out your monthly expenses can really open your eyes to exactly where you are spending your money and help you target areas to cut spending on. You can use a simple spreadsheet like the example below and group your expenses into broad categories using information from your bank and credit card statements. Here's an *example*[24] format that you can use:

---

[23] https://www.youneedabudget.com/
[24] http://www.fcac-acfc.gc.ca/Eng/resources/publications/budgeting/Pages/MakingaB-Commentf.aspx

Sample Budget - Source: Government of Canada	Previous month	Budget	Actual spending	Difference
INCOME				
Salary or benefits	3,000	3,000	3,000	0
Canada Child Tax Benefit (CCTB)				
Other				
TOTAL INCOME	2,500	2,500	2,500	0
BASIC EXPENSES (NEEDS)				
HOME				
Rent or mortgage payment	1,000	1,000	1,000	0
Property taxes/condo fees	50	50	50	0
Home insurance	100	100	100	0
Utilities (electricity, water, cable and/or telephone)	100	80	70	-10
Repairs and maintenance				
TRANSPORTATION				
Public transportation	230	250	220	-30
Car loan payment				
Car repairs, gas, etc.				
Car insurance/registration, etc.				
LIVING EXPENSES				
Groceries	250	200	180	-20
Child care				
Medical and dental	50	0	0	
Outstanding loan payments				
Basic clothing	120	50	0	-50
Life, disability and medical insurance				
Emergency fund				
Other				
OTHER EXPENSES (WANTS)				
Restaurants and entertainment	100	50	30	-20
Clothing (extra)				
Hair care				
Gifts	50	20	50	30
Vacations				
Other				
TOTAL EXPENSES	2,050	1,800	1,700	-100
SAVINGS (Total income minus total expenses)	450	700	800	100

Figure 21: The government of Canada's sample budget.

Right away, you're going to want to attack 'the big three': housing, transportation, and food. The traditional advice is to never spend more than 30% of your income on housing. This advice isn't completely practical because the cost of housing varies so significantly from city to city and increases seemingly every year. But do what you can to keep this number low. Living with a roommate or two will drastically decrease the amount of time it takes for you to become FI. Remain skeptical though. What if sharing a place or living in a cheaper area meant paying more to get to work? Costs of vehicle ownership—including gas, insurance, maintenance—as well as the cost of the car itself can really add up. A very common trend amongst people trying to achieve FI is to live close enough to work so that they don't need to own a car. Although this isn't practical everywhere, do consider if it would work for you. It's good for your wallet, your health, and the environment. Many, many couples across the United States are now realizing that having a second car isn't worth the extra years it means they'll have to work.

With respect to food costs, there's surprisingly just as much variance in the amount people spend on food as there is on transportation and housing. You can check out any newspaper's finance section to find horror stories of couples spending thousands of dollars a month on food and wine at restaurants. In the FI game, home cooking always wins. Skills like basic car maintenance, home cooking and meal prep, and knowing how to use a screwdriver can go a long way towards helping your budget.

Now, let's be clear. Going from two cars to one (or from one to zero) isn't easy. But these are the kind of sacrifices that most people have to make if they want to become FI in their thirties or forties.

The big three is often accompanied by a fourth big expense: health care. As a Canadian, I can't directly relate to the astronomical cost of medical treatment in the USA. Instead, I'll point you to some excellent blog posts that discuss health care options for early retirees: number one[25], and number two[26].

Is frugality a requirement for FI? No, absolutely not—the only requirement is having 25X your expenses. But frugality helps a lot. As we've discussed in the sub-chapter on "The Power of Saving," spending less is much more powerful than earning more. FI is about being super frugal in the same way that it's about saving tens of millions of dollars and only using a 1% savings withdrawal rate (SWR)—yes, it's an option. As long as you understand the impact of lifestyle

---

[25] https://livingafi.com/2016/11/11/obamacares-uncertain-future-and-the-impact-on-early-retirement-planning/

[26] http://rootofgood.com/obamacare_makes_early_retirement_easier_and_more_secure/

decisions on your finances, physical, and mental well-being, go ahead and plan for any type of FI that you'd like.

Once you get closer to FI and you've made some of the big decisions in your life (like if you'll have kids or what city you want to live in), you can get a more accurate idea of exactly how close you are to it. The best way to estimate your spending once you stop working is to take a prolonged sabbatical. A couple of months off can really tell you what you can expect your average spending to be. In the withdrawal stage, you might find that you spend a lot less on work clothes and transportation to work but more on leisure, travel, and hobbies. To track net worth, you can use popular programs like *Mint*[27] or *Personal Capital*[28]. Personally, I see little need for fancy programs that can be easily replicated by excel spreadsheets—but find the solution that's right for you.

A sabbatical of this nature would also tell you if you really want to be retired in the first place. Studies (albeit of varying and sometimes questionable quality) have shown that one's health often declines after leaving the work force. But don't let that be a reason to stop you—causality has not been proven in any of these studies. For most people, the sedentary lifestyle imposed by most white collar jobs is probably more of a health issue than the dreaded lack of purpose that some people fear will come with retirement. All in all, make sure you're retiring *to* something and *not just from* something. Have a plan and hobbies to stay busy.

What if everyone strives for FI?

If everyone in North America retired early, there would be an economic crisis of unprecedented proportions. Don't we need people to work and contribute to society? Don't we need people to consume a lot of stuff to ensure stock returns keep going up? Yes, it's true, if everyone adapted a FI mindset with a side of frugality, you wouldn't be able to rely on the Trinity Study or any other historical

---

[27] https://www.mint.com/
[28] https://www.personalcapital.com/

model to forecast your finances. When asked what normal Americans could do to help their country after 9/11, George Bush famously told people to go Disney World. Consumption is the lifeblood of capitalism.

Think about this the next time you try to get your extended family to agree on pizza toppings or to the date of a family reunion. It's incredibly difficult to get a large number of people to agree on *anything* trivial, let alone those bigger lifestyle questions like how much money they should spend. On the off chance that you could get everyone in the Western world to agree to live a frugal, anti-consumption lifestyle, let me know as there are a couple of other issues that could use your attention: you should get started right away on nuclear disarmament, reversing climate change, and banning Hawaiian pizza from existence.

Figure 22: The master negotiator.

Similarly, if everyone bought index tracking exchange traded funds, what would even be the point of the stock market? In this scenario, the market prices in an index would be solely driven by demand for investments, regardless of any individual company's prospects.

There are thousands of impacts that can be dreamt up about this and they're almost all negative, but that doesn't mean you should worry about it. There are enough pension funds, endowment funds, charities, universities, and other entities out there that have different investing needs than individuals do. Passive index investing will never be appropriate for most of these institutions. And don't forget: there are a massive number of actively managed investments in the industry and the huge number of day-traders in basements across the country trying to beat the markets. Don't worry and focus on your stress on something more productive.

Chapter 9

Asset allocation: Picking the right portfolio

We've talked about diversification and low-fee exchange traded funds (ETFs). We've talked about real estate, gold, and entrepreneurship. You know that you should probably have some bonds. You know that risk tolerance and time horizon are the key factors that should determine the percentage of equities in your portfolio. So, what should your portfolio look like?

Asset allocation, i.e. the percentage that each investment make-ups your total portfolio, can be as tough a nut to crack as you want it to be. There's no single correct or optimal answer. And there are many ways to get a diversified, inexpensive portfolio that can sustain the savings withdrawal rate (SWR)—of 4% or otherwise—that you'd choose. And yes, your way might even include real estate income trusts (REITs) or gold stocks.

But there are some ways that are decidedly more simple than others.

The first is to use a *target date fund*. A popular and extremely simple option, target date funds have names like "Target Retirement 2045." You put money into the fund when you can and everything else is taken care of for you. The percentage of equities that are American or emerging markets or whatever is determined by the fund administrator and the percentage of bonds in the portfolio increases as you get closer to the target date. Eventually, when the target date is reached, the fund will consist of around 40% bonds, or whatever other allocation the fund administrator has decided is appropriate for clients in the withdrawal stage. Re-balancing happens automatically and you have nothing to worry about, except for fees that are slightly higher than ETFs but still much cheaper than most actively managed mutual funds. These are a great option for anyone too nervous to truly do it themselves, but still wanting to get away from get away from ridiculously high fees.

A cheaper and more hands-on approach is the *classic three-fund portfolio*. This approach consists of three funds: domestic stocks, foreign stocks, and domestic bonds.

The first big question is, how you should split your equities between domestic and foreign? If you're American, you might see that American stock markets make up 55% of the world's market cap and aim for something around that percentage. Similar to how overweighing gold stocks (relative to their size in the market) adds risk to your portfolio, it can be argued that overweighing one's country's stocks has the same effect.

But there are also arguments that Americans should overweigh the equities of their home country: if you pay your bills in American dollars, you don't want your investments to fluctuate in value too much due to changes in currency values. And American stocks are taxed more favourably for American residents, so why not take advantage? Again, there's no single 'one-fits-all' answer but it is a good idea to include *some* international stocks in order to achieve true diversification. America had great growth in the 20th century but what if most of the growth in the 21st century is experienced by other countries? You wouldn't want to miss out on that. Don't over-think it. Target somewhere between 55% and 80% *of your equities* (not necessarily your entire portfolio) to be American and move on.

The second question and final question often asked regarding the three-fund approach is, what percentage of bonds do I want in my asset allocation? Recall from our discussion on bonds above, that the percentage bonds you want is primarily determined by the flexibility of your timeline to financial independence (FI) and how much of a ride (ups and downs) you're willing to take along the way. An equity-heavy portfolio means that you have to be okay with delaying your time to FI if market conditions so dictate. For example, a person who wants to be aggressive in their timeline to FI and is very flexible might have the following portfolio:

Asset	Allocation
American Equity ETF	60%
International Equity ETF	30%
American Bond ETF	10%

Figure 23: Three fund approach, aggressive.

Of course, you could decide to have 0% bonds or even a small-cap tilt, but that wouldn't be a simple, low-maintenance, three-fund approach. Those high risk asset allocations aren't for most people. The majority of investors will want at least 10% bonds in order to take advantage of re-balancing. If someone using the three-fund approach wants a more predictable timeline to FI, they might have the following portfolio:

Asset	Allocation
American Equity ETF	50%
International Equity ETF	20%
American Bond ETF	30%

Figure 24: Three fund approach, balanced.

It doesn't matter tremendously if you have 50% American equities or 55% in the above scenario. The most important thing is that once you pick an allocation you stick to it. Don't change it every year or every time you read something in the news about the stock market. Changing your allocation too often undermines your portfolio and can put your plan in jeopardy.

In order to determine whether you need an aggressive, moderate, or conservative portfolio to reach your FI goals, you should consider the following:

• Current savings rate

• Current net worth

• Expected annual return on investment

- Withdrawal rate

- Flexibility of your plan and personal risk tolerance

Do some research on the expected returns of your portfolio for the time horizon you plan to accumulate funds for and enter your information into a calculator—like the one on *http://NetWorthify.com*—to see what kind of results you get. If the results aren't to your liking, you can change one or more of the variables listed above until you find an outcome that matches your preferences.

This discussion has been about asset allocation in the accumulation stage but don't get rid of all your equities once you're in the withdrawal stage. The Trinity Study was conducted with a 60/40 split between equity and bonds, but you can run your own simulations to determine portfolio success rates using *http://cfiresim.com*. The one thing you will find from these simulations is that your portfolio success rates start to go downhill quickly if you hold more than 40% bonds. You need the growth that equities provide to sustain a savings withdrawal rate (SWR) of 4%, especially if you intend to retire early.

Although the traditional advice offered to retirees is to hold a lot of bonds (or other fixed income products) there is evidence that this may not be an optimal solution. A *study*[29] released by Pfau and Kitces in 2013 looked at using a *rising equity glide-path* in retirement. The pair found that increasing equity exposure throughout retirement led to higher portfolio success rates because it helped to mitigate the sequence of returns risk (i.e. bad equity returns in the beginning of the withdrawal stage). By increasing equity exposure every year in retirement, retirees that retired "at a bad time" are sheltered from equities in the critical early years of withdrawal and exposed to equities when the good returns manifest. This is only one, rather non-traditional, way of organizing your portfolio in the withdrawal stage but it's worthy of consideration. Research it and other options and make sure to run your own simulations at *http://cfiresim.com*

This has been a brief overview on one of the simpler methods (and tools) for investors to design a low-fee and diversified portfolio for themselves. As long as

---

[29] https://papers.ssrn.com/sol3/papers.cfm?abstract_id=2324930

you re-balance regularly (1-2 times a year is fine) and don't change your allocation based on market events, the three-fund approach is a great option. If you're considering adding additional assets to your portfolio, check out *Portfolio Charts*[30] which beautifully displays data on other simple approaches that have been popularized throughout the years, including their historical SWRs. Just keep in mind that these other approaches can add complexity, time, and (sometimes) fees. The three-fund approach should be considered by everyone trying to do, but not overdo, it themselves.

Asset allocation for Canadians

Unfortunately, target date funds are not widely available, nor inexpensive, outside of America. But this is changing. For those of us outside of the world's largest economy, the three-fund approach is our best option, but extra considerations that need to be taken into account. Numerous reports estimate that most Canadians allocate somewhere around 60% of their equities to Canadian stocks. This is known as *home country bias* and it describes the tendency of investors to overweigh (i.e. hold too much of) the stocks of their home country, even if their home country (like Canada) makes up only a tiny fraction of the total world stock market (around 4%) and is mostly made up of natural resource and banking stocks.

There are some legitimate reasons to have a home country bias. Like we discussed above, domestic stocks usually get favourable tax treatment and there's no risk that changes in currency exchange rates will impact the value of your investments. But it's safe to say that investors holding 60% of their investments in small stock markets like Canada or Australia are not getting enough diversification. Unfortunately, this is another aspect of investing where there is no clear "right" answer. But Canadian investors can reasonably defend an allocation that has anywhere from 4-30% of Canadian equity even given that Canada.

---

[30] https://portfoliocharts.com/portfolios/

Like the three-fund approach for non-American investors, your portfolio will still include domestic stocks, foreign stocks, and domestic bonds. The difference is that foreign stocks are targeted with a higher allocation. But, like Americans, the percentage of bonds held by non-Americans will still be dependent on the risks you're willing to take and the flexibility of your timeline to financial independence (FI). A Canadian with a goal of becoming FI in 25 years with minimal changes to a three-fund plan might have the following portfolio:

Asset	Allocation
Canadian Equity ETF	20%
All-World Ex-Canada ETF (every stock market other than Canada)	50%
Canada Bond ETF	30%

Figure 25: Three fund approach, balanced.

If this same individual determined that, with their current savings rate, achieving FI might be difficult in 25 years unless they achieved some very good returns and they are okay with moving their target date up or back by more than a couple of years, their portfolio might look like this:

Asset	Allocation
Canadian Equity ETF	30%
All-World Ex-Canada ETF (Every stock market other than Canada)	60%
Canada Bond ETF	10%

Figure 26: Three fund approach, aggressive.

The three-fund approach is great. It's relatively cheap and easy to re-balance. (Just don't forget to do so on a regular schedule!) But if you're in search of a more optimal or tax-efficient portfolio, things become a bit more complicated.

One way to do this is to hold more funds, instead of just an All-World Ex-Canada ETF. By breaking this fund up into smaller pieces, like an Emerging Markets and European ETF, you'll get lower fees. But you'll still have to consider other factors like foreign currency risk and withholding taxes for those holding significant portions of their portfolios in foreign currencies. You can see a more detailed discussion on this in Appendix H: Is currency risk a part of a diversified portfolio?

Putting your assets in their place: A necessary blurb on taxes

Each country has its own *tax-advantaged* accounts. Governments create these accounts to give people incentives to save for their own retirement. After all, the system doesn't want to be on the hook for everything when you're older. Tax-advantaged accounts are simply containers and what you put in the container, usually stocks and bonds, is up to you. (For the most part, that is.) An important question to consider is, "What 'container' or type of account should I put my investments in?" Knowing the rules and strengths and weaknesses of different types of accounts can save you some real time towards achieving financial independence (FI), so it's probably worth taking 5 minutes to learn the basics.

In order to navigate the different types of retirement accounts available to you, you'll need to understand the very basics of the taxation system. First, there's an all too common misconception (sometimes sneakily whispered by employers) that if you get a promotion and make a higher salary, you might actually end up taking home *less* money at the end of the day because you got bumped into a higher tax bracket. Let's be totally clear here: this is a factually impossible scenario in a 21st century western country. The modern income tax system is progressive and uses marginal rates, not flat rates. This means that, for example, on your *first* $15,000 earned, you pay X%, and on your *second* $15,000 earned, you pay X% + 10%, and so on.

Your *marginal tax rate* is the amount you pay on any new income you earn: i.e. the X% that you pay on the next Y dollars that you earn. Your *effective tax rate* is the average rate at which you're taxed: i.e. your total tax paid divided by your tax total income for the year. Other than tax-advantaged retirement accounts, normal investing accounts are 'taxable accounts' because they don't have the tax advantages.

Also, you should know that there are three different types of income you're typically going to receive from stocks and bonds. Bonds produce *interest* income in the form of regularly scheduled cash payments to you. Stocks produce *capital gains* when you sell them for more than you bought them for, and *dividends* usually when a company decides to write you a cheque because they been profitable and want to reward your loyalty.

Investment accounts and brokerages in the USA

In America, accounts come in two flavors: traditional and Roth. *Traditional accounts* are funded with pre-tax income, meaning you pay less tax in the year that you contribute to the account but have to pay tax on your withdrawals from the account. *Roth accounts*, on the other hand, are funded with after-tax income and, because you've already paid, you don't pay taxes on your withdrawals. The standard advice is to use a traditional account if you have a high marginal tax rate and expect to be in a lower marginal tax bracket late. This is weighted so that you can to pay the IRS less money. This works well for people who are high earners now but expect to live off relatively little in retirement. And to add a bit more complication, the most popular accounts, 401ks and IRAs, both come in traditional and Roth flavours. It is worth it then to figure out which one is better suited to your tastes.

A *401k is an employer-provided defined contribution pension plan*—wait, don't fall asleep on me yet! Contributions to a 401k are usually taken off your pay before you even see it but they're still an important part of your compensation. If a 401k is available in your workplace, make sure you're signed up for it. And you have the option to set what percent of your paycheck you contribute, so the question is, "how much should you contribute?" You should *at least* match the amount that your employer is willing pay. If your employer says that they will match the first 3%, that means you will contribute 3% of your base salary in a year and they match it with the same contribution. That's a 100% return you just earned by doing nothing. It's also useful to note that the contribution limit or ceiling doesn't carry forward to the next year, meaning you'll lose it if you don't use it. So, make sure you use it if you can.

That said, after matching your employer's ceiling, don't contribute more than the limit ($18,000 in 2016) or you'll risk getting penalized by the IRS. Money in your 401k isn't intended to be withdrawn until you're 59.5 years old or you risk getting penalized by the IRS. There are legal ways to get around this penalty but they are outside the scope of this book. Suffice to say, that many resources are available to you. For example, the Internal Revenue Services (IRS) does a surprisingly decent job of explaining different tax-advantaged accounts on its *website*[31] and this *blog post*[32] provides a fantastic explanation of the "Roth Conversion Ladder"needed to avoid the 10% penalty on withdrawals before age 59.5. The Roth Conversion ladder is an incredibly powerful tool for early retirees in the United Stages, and I urge you to read that blog post from Justin's Root of Good blog if you plan on using it.

The *individual retirement account* (IRA) is another incredibly popular tax-advantaged account that you can open at any bank or financial institution. Unlike a 401k, you can contribute to one of these from your bank account instead of it coming off your pay check before you see the cash. The limit was $5,500 (combined for all IRAs you have, including Roth and Traditional) in 2016 and if you don't use all of that room by April 15, 2017, it's gone forever. Something else to keep in mind is that if you make over a certain amount of income, then you can't contribute to a Roth IRA; traditional IRAs are your only option. Your eligibility is determined by your *Modified Adjusted Gross Income* (MAGI). In 2015, single tax filers with MAGIs of $116,000 or more, and joint filers with MAGIs of $183,000 or more, were severely limited in the amount they could contribute to a Roth IRA. However, a popular way to get around is by opening a *Backdoor Roth IRA*[33].

As you know, IRAs come in both Roth and traditional flavours and deciding which one is right for you primarily depends on your expected future income

---

[31] https://www.irs.gov/retirement-plans/plan-sponsor/types-of-retirement-plans-1
[32] http://rootofgood.com/roth-ira-conversion-ladder-early-retirement/
[33] https://www.bogleheads.org/wiki/Backdoor_Roth_IRA

and tax rate. People earning income in high tax rates usually prefer traditional IRAs as it allows them to defer tax until later during the withdrawal phase. Their hope is that when they go to withdraw from their 401k, they'll benefit from being in a lower tax bracket. Effectively, they hope to save the difference between their tax rate when they contribute and when they withdraw. Determining what the better choice is in your personal situation can get complicated. Here's *a good discussion*[34] which goes into some more detail.

Note that your 401k is not an investment in and of itself – you need to choose what investment funds to use within the container that is your 401kk. The funds available in your 401k—as stocks and bonds—can vary drastically in fees. If your only options are funds with high expenses, talk to your workplace plan administrator. They're usually willing to add more funds at your request and the lack is usually due to the fact that people rarely ask for more options. Keep it simple and, like we've already discussed, invest in low-fee, broad-based index tracking exchange traded funds (ETFs) like those offered by Vanguard, Fidelity, or Blackrock.

Tax efficient fund placement in the USA

To make sure we're all on the same page: There are three different types of income you're typically going to receive from stocks and bonds. Bonds produce interest income in the form of regularly scheduled cash payments to you. Stocks produce capital gains when you sell them for more than you bought them for, and dividends usually when a company decides to write you a cheque because they have been profitable and want to reward your loyalty.

As a general 'rule of thumb', bonds are generally less tax-efficient than equities. Due to the fact that bonds receive interest income often (usually every month) and in a taxable investment account, you end up having to pay tax on that income. In comparison, equities funds are usually viewed as more tax-efficient

---

[34]

http://www.reddit.com/r/personalfinance/comments/2jqnjy/can_we_talk_a bout_the_misconceptions_people_have/

because you don't need to pay capital gains taxes until you sell your investment. Basically, bonds lose out on some compound returns because they get taxed more often. Equities also have other tax advantages: if you have *qualified dividends*[35], or *long-term capital gains*[36], they will be taxed at lower rates.

So, what does this all mean? Now, what 'container' should we place our investments in?

A traditional account treats all withdrawals as income and 100% of it is taxable at your marginal tax rate. Traditional accounts don't differentiate based on whether the dividends were qualified or your capital gains were long-term, so you lose those benefits if you hold stocks in them. For this reason, you can prioritize holding onto your bonds in retirement, tax advantaged accounts. Interest from bonds are always taxed at 100%, so your capital gains and dividends are treated essentially like interest income if you hold them in a traditional retirement account. (Another 'rule of thumb': it's almost always a good idea to use up your tax-advantaged room first, no matter what you're putting in it, before you switch to a normal taxable account!)

If you're following the approach of holding at least three funds, it's important to think, "in which accounts, or containers, will you be putting each fund?" Most people keep their bonds in a traditional account because 100% of interest earned from bonds is taxable whether they're in a traditional or a taxable account; they're tax-inefficient so it makes sense to keep them in a tax-advantaged account. This is preferable to keeping equities in a traditional account because, as we discussed above, capital gains and dividends are given preferential treatment in taxable accounts.

Additionally, people usually put their riskiest assets (meaning equities) in a Roth account. This is because the growth achieved by assets in Roth account is never taxed and people expect their riskiest assets to achieve the most growth. That said, if you have international equities (i.e. stocks from countries outside of the US), you may lose some foreign tax credits if you keep those equities in a tax-advantaged account. For this reason, it's a good idea to keep international

---

[35] https://www.bogleheads.org/wiki/Qualified_dividend
[36] https://www.bogleheads.org/wiki/Capital_gains_distribution

equities in a normal, taxable account if you've already used up all of your room in tax-advantaged accounts.

So how much exposure to international equities should you have in your portfolio?

There are different schools of thoughts on this subject. Some people say not to hold any stocks outside of the S&P 500. They argue that all of those huge companies are international anyways. If they can earn revenue around the world, isn't it basically the same as being exposed to the entire world's economy? Well, no. This seemingly compelling argument doesn't account for the fact that the total US stock market only accounts for 55% of the world's market cap. And yes, while the US experienced huge amounts of growth in the 20th century, don't limit yourself from taking advantage of similar growth spurts taking place in other countries through the 21st century.

And at the end of the day, when 55% of your equities are American equities, aren't you betting that they will out-perform the rest of the market on a risk-adjusted and long-term basis?

You can make a case here for supporting a home country bias. After all, you buy groceries and gas in American dollars. You pay taxes in American dollars. Don't you want to be able to plan for those expenses, instead of having wild fluctuations in your portfolio due to changes in exchange rates? Yes, you would, but there's no 'one-size fits all' answer here. You should have some international stocks but (arguably) not more than 45% of the equity portion of your portfolio. For further research, here is link to learn more about *where you should put your international equities*[37].

This has been a brief overview of the tax-advantaged accounts available to Americans and a quick look at the theory on where to keep your assets in a tax-efficient manner. As a starting point, make use of some of the valuable links that I've left above. Check them out. They'll be very useful to get you thinking about personalizing the advice here to your individual needs.

---

[37] https://www.bogleheads.org/wiki/Tax-efficient_fund_placement#Step_3:_Placing_international_stock_funds_in_the_taxable_account

Furthermore, here are a couple of very attractive account options that we didn't discuss above. One that you could consider using is the *Health Savings Account*[38] from which withdrawals can be made tax-free if they're for health reasons. For the self-employed, the *Individual 401k*[39], or *Mega Backdoor IRA*[40] (no, that's not the name of a rollercoaster), are two interesting and relevant account options.

Addendum: Conventional wisdom has recently been turned on its head. You may have noticed or heard that bonds have been returning low amounts of interest in the last half-decade or so. That's because central banks have decreased interest rates in order to make borrowing cheaper and to spur the economy. These super-low returns from bonds means that they may actually be more tax-efficient in a taxable account than equities. The thinking is that even if interest income is tax-inefficient, there will be so little of it that it won't really matter. Proponents of this idea don't want to waste tax-efficient space in an 401(k) or IRA on an investment product (bonds) that really doesn't seem to be doing much for them lately. Indications from federal governments in 2016 indicate that this low-rate environment is likely to persist for some time longer, meaning this may remain a viable strategy for the foreseeable future.

Investment accounts and brokerages in Canada

The *Tax-Free Savings Account* (TFSA) is arguably the worst misnomer in Canadian investment history because it's not actually a product by itself—or a "savings account" for that matter—it's a 'container'. The TFSA is a tax-advantaged account or container where you can put cash (i.e. treat it like a savings account), mutual funds, or other stock/bond funds. The big banks make TFSAs even more confusing than they need to be by splitting them up into different types of TFSAs but it's all just marketing speech. Tell them you want a *self-directed TFSA* and get set up to invest in low-fee exchange traded funds

---

[38] https://www.bogleheads.org/wiki/Health_savings_account
[39] https://en.wikipedia.org/wiki/Solo_401(k)
[40] http://whitecoatinvestor.com/the-mega-backdoor-roth-ira/

(ETFs). Or better yet, start your TFSA at a discount broker like *Questrade*[41], *Virtual Brokers*[42], or *Qtrade*[43].

To be clear, you want a TFSA. It is as good of an investment option as it is an atrocious example of obfuscating investment-speak. Any income you earn on amounts you put in your TFSA will never be taxable and it also doesn't count as income that makes you be less eligible for government programs like *Old Age Security*. In 2016, the contribution room for residents (over 18 years of age) was $5,500 but, before you limit yourself, check if you have old contribution room that you haven't used yet. Contribution room never expires and if you withdraw from your TFSA, it doesn't reduce how much you can carry forward and contribute in the future. That means, for example, if your investments in your TFSA were to grow to one million dollars and you decide to withdraw it, then your contribution room would become one million dollars.

TFSAs were new on the scene in 2009, so most Canadians are more familiar with the other big tax-advantaged accounts such as the mainstay *Registered Retirement Savings Plan* (RRSP) and the *Registered Pension Plan* (RPP). Your RRSP/RPP contribution room (like your TFSA room) doesn't expire and instead of a set amount every year, your room is based on how much you earn and the lower option of either: 1) 18% of your earned income in the previous year (which excludes dividends and capital gains) or 2) the annual limit (which was $25,370 in 2016). The big difference between the TFSA and RRSP is that you contribute after-tax money to a TFSA and you aren't taxed on withdrawal, whereas an RRSP you contribute pre-tax money and you are taxed on withdrawal. What this means is that if you do decide to contribute after-tax money to your RRSP from your paycheque, you'll get a tax deduction and possibly a refund when you file your taxes.

RPPs function similar to an RRSP but are organized through your employer and an administrator they hire like Great West Life, Sun Life, or Manulife. They use same contribution room as RRSPs, so make sure you don't go over the limit! RPP often include funds with nasty high expenses and poor selection but that is

---

[41] http://www.questrade.com/
[42] https://www.virtualbrokers.com/en-us/
[43] https://www.qtrade.ca/

made up for the fact that employers sometimes offer a "match." If the match is 100% up to 3% of your salary, that means that if you put, say, 2.5% of your paycheque into a RPP, your employer will kick in the same amount. This is a huge bonus; think of it as a 100% instant return on your investment. It doesn't matter what kind of funds are in your RPP, make sure you're contributing at least up to the match!

So, what is better: the RRSP or TFSA? Let's keep it simple. The main benefit of the RRSP is that if you are in a higher tax bracket when you take the RRSP deduction (compared to when you make the withdrawal), you effectively eliminate the difference in taxes. To clarify: let's say that you decide to make a $1,000 RRSP deduction when you are in a 50% marginal tax bracket. That means you will reduce your tax owed in that year by $500. If you are in a 30% marginal tax bracket when you take out that $1,000, you only have to pay $300. This means that you will have saved paying $200 of income tax to the government. Notice that I said *deduction* here and not contribution. You're not required to take the tax deduction in the same year that you make the RRSP contribution to the account.

The most appropriate investment is probably clear to you. If you are in a high tax bracket right now, go with the RRSP before you fund your TFSA. Of course, it's hard to be totally certain that you'll be in a lower tax bracket in retirement. If you're not sure, there's nothing wrong with prioritizing your TFSA. It's a great account and you can't go wrong with it. Once you've maxed out your TFSA and RRSP, you can open up a normal taxable account or perhaps a *Registered Education Savings Plan* (RESP) if you want to partially fund your kids' education.

Tax efficient fund placement in Canada

To make sure we're all on the same page: There are three different types of income you're typically going to receive from stocks and bonds. Bonds produce interest income in the form of regularly scheduled cash payments to you. Stocks produce capital gains when you sell them for more than you bought them for, and dividends usually when a company decides to write you a cheque because they have been profitable and want to reward your loyalty.

Before we start investing, just as in the American scenario above, let's look at the types of income generated by bonds and stocks with an eye on tax-efficiency. As a general rule of thumb, bonds are generally less tax-efficient than equities. This is because bonds produce income from interest often (usually every month) and in a taxable investment account, you have to pay tax on that income. Equities are usually viewed as more tax-efficient because you don't need to pay capital gains taxes until you sell your investment. Basically, bonds lose out on some compound returns because they get taxed more often.

Equities have other tax-advantages too. Only 50% of capital gains are taxable as opposed to 100% of interest income. That doesn't meant that you have to pay 50% tax on capital gains – it means only 50% *of* your capital gains can get taxed. For example, if you bought stocks for $100 and sold them for $500, you have a $400 capital gain. 50% of that $400, or $200, is taxable. If your marginal tax rate is 30%, the actual tax you end up paying would be $60 (30% X $200). Dividends get special treatment also. If the dividends are from a Canadian company, you get a tax credit that makes them approximately equal to capital gains in terms of total cost incurred in tax.

In terms of tax-efficiency, the three-fund approach is easy to optimize. All withdrawals from an RRSP are 100% taxable. This means that the favourable tax treatment of dividends and capital gains is lost in this account. Because of this, it makes sense to put your bond funds in your RRSP, where everything would be treated like interest income anyways. Withdrawals from your TFSA, on the other hand, are 100% tax free. That means you should put your riskiest assets – equities – in there so that they can grow unrestrained. Canadian-listed exchange traded funds (ETFs) that hold foreign stocks are a good option to keep in the TFSA. And finally, the dividends from Canadian corporations are taxed at favourable rates so they're a good option to put in your taxable account, assuming that you don't have any RRSP or TFSA room left.

In summary, someone following the three-fund approach may try to prioritize their investments in the following manner:

RRSP – Canadian Bond ETF

TFSA –All-World Ex-Canada ETF (trades on the TSX)

Taxable Account – Canadian Equities ETF

If you want to optimize your portfolio to have the lowest fees and taxes, you're going to have to split your holdings into more ETFs. The smaller ETFs, like the ones for emerging markets or developed countries outside of North America, hold fewer companies and thus have lower fees than the ETFs that track bigger parts of the world.

A portfolio with more funds should try to avoid withholding taxes on foreign dividends. When you get dividends from foreign countries, including the US, the Americans levy a withholding tax of up to 15% of your dividend. This means that investors following the three-fund approach might be missing out on a sizable portion of their dividends from their All-World Ex-Canada ETF. That said, if you hold your funds with foreign dividends in a taxable account you may likely recover those amounts on line 405 of your tax return by entering it as a federal foreign tax credit. Something is better than nothing, right?

One way to get around the foreign withholding tax from the United States is to hold the *US-listed ETFs*—i.e. ones that trade on the *New York Stock Exchange*—instead of the equivalent ETF that trades on the *TSX*. With these US-listed ETFs in an RRSP, the withholding tax is not applicable due to an agreement between the two countries, so you can avoid it all together. The downside is that you end up paying for the currency exchange, which can be expensive, but if our main objective is to have low fees, this is the way to go.

Addendum: Conventional wisdom has recently been turned on its head. You may have noticed or heard that bonds have been returning low amounts of interest in the last half-decade or so. That's because central banks have decreased interest rates in order to make borrowing cheaper and to spur the economy. These super-low returns from bonds means that they may actually be more tax-efficient in a taxable account than equities. The thinking is that even if interest income is tax-inefficient, there will be so little of it that it won't really matter. Proponents of this idea don't want to waste tax-efficient space in an

RRSP or TFSA on an investment product (bonds) that really doesn't seem to be doing much for them lately. Indications from federal governments in 2016 indicate that this low-rate environment is likely to persist for some time longer, meaning this may remain a viable strategy for the foreseeable future.

Chapter 10

Priorities for wealth and happiness

Where to put your savings: Canada

All of the details can be confusing. Here are some step-by-step instructions on where to put your savings. These were originally intended to be presented in a nice flow chart as opposed to text. You can find the flowchart versions on my blog www.graemefalco.com for quick reference.

1. Emergency fund. Keep 3-6 months worth of expenses in a high interest savings account for things like major car, home, or dental repairs. At a certain point, say once you also have 3-6 months worth of expenses in your investment accounts, you may not see the need for an e-fund anymore. You can use credit cards and lines of credit in the event of an emergency. It only takes a couple of days to sell and transfer assets from your brokerage's taxable account to you chequing account. Your comfort level with an emergency fund is totally personal and there's nothing wrong with having a large one - but if it's more than 6 months' worth of expenses you're missing out on investment returns that money could be earning for you.

2. Employer plan to match. Contribute to your company's RRSP/RPP to get the employer's full match. The match is an instant 100% return!

3. Debt. Paying off debt is amazing because it is a guaranteed return. It's one of the only free lunches you can find in the world of investing! Make sure to read the earlier sub-chapter on Stomping out the debt monster.

4. Tax-advantaged accounts. Contribute to your RRSP and TFSA, prioritizing based on your expected future tax brackets. The RRSP is the better option if you'll be in a lower tax bracket in the the withdrawal stage than you are in the accumulation stage, and the TFSA is the better option in almost all other possible scenarios. If you're planning on funding your child's education, you can also contribute to a *Registered Education Savings Plan* in this step.

5. Taxable accounts. Contribute anything that doesn't fit into your RRSP or TFSA into a normal, taxable, investing account. You can open one at any of the big banks or popular discount brokerages like Questrade and Virtual Brokers.

Where to put your savings: USA

All of the details can be confusing. Here are some step-by-step instructions on where to put your savings. These were originally intended to be presented in a nice flow chart as opposed to text. You can find the flowchart versions on my blog www.graemefalco.com for quick reference.

1. Emergency fund. Keep 3-6 months worth of expenses in a high interest savings account for things like major car, home, or dental repairs. At a certain point, say once you also have 3-6 months worth of expenses in your investment accounts, you may not see the need for an e-fund anymore. You can use credit cards and lines of credit in the event of an emergency. It only takes a couple of days to sell and transfer assets from your brokerage's taxable account to you chequing account. Your comfort level with an emergency fund is totally personal and there's nothing wrong with having a large one - but if it's more than 6 months' worth of expenses you're missing out on investment returns that money could be earning for you.

2. Employer plan to match. Contribute to your 401(k) (or 403(b) or 457(b)) to take advantage of the full match offered by your employer. The match is an instant 100% return!

3. Debt. Paying off debt is amazing because it is a guaranteed return. It's one of the only free lunches you can find in the world of investing! Make sure to read the earlier sub-chapter on Stomping out the debt monster.

4. Health Savings Account (HSA). Contribute to a HSA if you're eligible for one (I.e. your health insurance is a qualified high deductible health plan). Because you have a high deductible, you want to be ready to cover costs in the case of a medical emergency.,

5. Individual Retirement Account (IRA). Contribute to an IRA if you're eligible to. A traditional IRA is the better option if you expect your future tax bracket in the withdrawal stage to be a lower one than your tax bracket in the accumulation stage. In most other situations, Roth IRAs are the better option. We discussed whether or not you're eligible for a Roth IRA in the chapter on Asset Allocation: Picking the right portfolio.

6. Remainder of Employer Plan. Contribute the rest of what you can to your workplace plan. Whether it's a traditional or Roth plan will again depend on your earning and spending situation.

7. Taxable accounts. Contribute anything that doesn't fit in any of the above containers to a normal, taxable investing account that you can open at any one of the big banks or popular discount brokerages.

Do retirement accounts like the 401(k) lock you in to them and penalize you heavily if you try to withdraw from them before you're 59.5 years old? They *can,* but there are legal and common ways around it. I'd like to take this opportunity to remind you of this *blog post*[44], which provides a fantastic explanation of the "Roth Conversion Ladder" needed to avoid the 10% penalty on withdrawals

---

[44] http://rootofgood.com/roth-ira-conversion-ladder-early-retirement/

before age 59.5. The Roth Conversion ladder is an incredibly powerful tool for early retirees in the United Stages, and I urge you to read that blog post from Justin's Root of Good blog if you are interested in retiring before your 60th birthday.

Don't burn out on FI

All too often people think that achieving financially independent (FI) will allow them to become the person they are really meant to be. But just as buying physical objects can't make you happy in the long run, a big pile of investments can't give you self-esteem or satisfaction from life.

Delayed gratification is a major part of becoming FI but that doesn't mean that you shouldn't allow yourself to live in the present. Some people work so hard to achieve FI that they forget who they really are and their hobbies and friendships fade away. I once had someone tell me that he thought he would feel good about himself once he reached $500K in his investment accounts and was surprised when he didn't feel that way. Instead of taking an objective look at himself, he muttered "maybe it will happen when I'm actually retired."

Other than coming to terms with how desperately he needs a vacation, this person needed to realize that being miserable in the accumulation stage of FI usually means being miserable afterwards. Sure, it's exciting now; after you've read a few books and blogs about ways to increase your savings rate, all that's left to do is, well, save. And wait. And then - wait some more. You don't want to lament about how long that middle part of the journey is. That so-called 'middle part' is your life. You would be best served by learning to enjoy it. Live it to the fullest and do all the things you would do if you were retired in FI; but in smaller, weekend-sized batches. Besides, as the old adage says, if you retire *from* something instead of *to* something, you're going to have a miserable time.

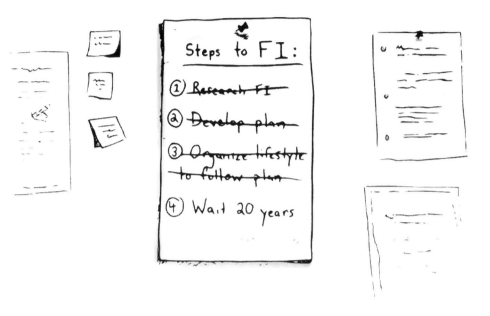

Figure 27: The "saving and waiting" part of FI is long. It's also your life, so learn to enjoy it.

Don't use the pursuit of FI as a crutch for your emotional well-being. Instead, take time to take care of your mental and physical health. What good is the freedom of being FI if you're never able to fully enjoy it? Yes, don't miss out on this incredible opportunity to be FI because it's a rare one that most people in the world will never get to consider but don't lose sight of what it's about. Make decisions that not only are the right decisions from a long-term financial perspective but also from the perspective of quality of life and total happiness.

One of the most famous studies on happiness was conducted at Harvard Medical School and is called the Grant Study. It tracked 268 men over a 75 year time period, including former U.S. President John F. Kennedy. Universally, the study found that the happiest people were the ones with the most positive and deep personal relationships. These were not the wealthiest or most prestigious subjects of the study; they were the subjects that developed a mental perspective that allowed them to be happy. FI will not make you content. But FI may give you the time and resources you need to develop a content perspective. It's up to you to ensure that FI is a positive, enabling force in your life, and not a distraction, obsession, or roadblock.

The end

Thanks for reading! That's the entirety of this book. I hope you learned something and enjoyed it. If you did, please continue reading the appendices. Some topics, like Appendix B: The pitfalls of dividend investing and Appendix H: Is currency risk a part of a diversified portfolio?, were too long or complicated to include in the body of the book, but are absolutely worth reading. Others, like Appendix D: The Peak Doom Phenomenon and Appendix F: Automation and the future of jobs, were just too fun to write and couldn't be left out.

I am not infallible by any means. However, the majority of my beliefs and analyses are backed by academic research, corroborated through the scientific method. If you have any counterpoints or points of discussion that are based on empirical evidence, I would love to hear it. Please contact me at graemecpa@gmail.com.

Follow me on twitter @graemeCPA, and reddit /u/graemeCPA. You can also join my mailing list[45] or visit www.graemefalco.com.

---

[45] http://eepurl.com/coq6IL

Appendices

Appendix A: Green funds and fossil fuel divestment

Is it just a coincidence that not indulging in materialistic consumption can be a boon towards your financial independence (FI) goals as well as lowering your carbon footprint? Are stock investments and environmentally conscious living antithetical?

Anyone who has seen the data on climate change should be a proponent of living a low-carbon lifestyle and overall environmental stewardship. Daily carbon levels in the atmosphere are over 400 parts per million—you can see the daily carbon rating posted at *http://www.co2.earth*. This is a particularly bad sign because the last time carbon levels were this high, humans didn't exist. And yes, there is *overwhelming consensus among scientists*[46] that it is extremely likely that climate change is due to human activity.

Now, let's be clear about what climate change is and isn't. Climate change is not about the death of all humans, one-time weather events, or a conspiracy to get you to pay more for high-efficiency light bulbs. It is, however, very specifically about an average increase in the Earth's temperature; and so, it is also about the extinction of many animals and plants, rising water levels, and a *multiplier of*

---

[46] http://climate.nasa.gov/scientific-consensus/

risk[47] on a wide range of potential crises. Given that bleak picture, should you invest in exchange traded funds (ETFs) that exclude the world's biggest carbon polluting companies?

The answer depends what your goal is in doing so. Many people buy green or low-carbon ETFs because they don't want to support or finance the big polluters but the stock market is a secondary market. This means that when you buy a stock, your money doesn't go directly to that company's bank account; instead, your money goes to the person you bought it from. The benefit to the company is indirect and minimal.

So, is it worth it? What are the drawbacks of this strategy?

1. Fees: Any socially responsible fund is going to be somewhat actively managed. This means higher fees than a truly passive index. As you know from reading about money managers in general, even the smallest fees means adding months or years to the road to financial independence (FI number).

2. Lack of diversification: By now you know that including any group of stocks over another in your portfolio adds non-systematic risk, regardless of what differentiates the groups. Having a green bias in your investments will increase the volatility of your investments. For example, if a country found oil reserves underground this could lead to a decrease in the price and your investments could take a big hit. And what about the banks that loan money to fossil fuel companies? Will you try to divest from every low-carbon industry that supplies or interacts with a high carbon one? The implications of an environmentally friendly approach to investing depend on how far you take it. For example, investing in nothing but the renewable energy sector would result in an incredibly volatile portfolio. It would be an understatement to say that a 4% savings withdrawal rate (SWR) rate would no longer apply to your case.

For most individuals, low-carbon investments are likely to be more symbolic than anything else. Some people absolutely refuse to be a cog in the wheel of (what they perceive to be) a morally bankrupt system and that's a position that I

---

[47] https://climateandsecurity.files.wordpress.com/2012/04/climate-change-as-threat-multiplier_understanding-the-broader-nature-of-the-risk_briefer-252.pdf

empathize with. I understand if some people are personally able to justify such a position. Anyone who does this should understand that it will severely delay their time to FI and that there are likely many easier ways to support the cause and make more of an impactful difference.

This isn't a treatise on how to live a low-carbon lifestyle but I will add that, if you look around, you'll find plenty of more effective tools to living that ethical, eco-life than expensive green investments. Eating less meat, driving your car less, or buying local food will do better for the world than divesting from fossil fuels. If you want to make the world a better place, the best recommendation I can give you is to invest using a broad-based index approach and retire early. The increased diversification that you can achieve with a broad-based fund means that you will increase the likelihood of retiring earlier and actively doing more tangible good for the world's carbon problem than a green fund investment strategy could ever do.

Appendix B: The pitfalls of dividend investing

It's a big, scary, and efficient market out there, boy-o! That means that investors already expect dividend paying companies to keep paying dividends and that is already priced into the stock price. Uh-oh.

Dividends are in fact one of the most commonly misunderstood aspects of investing. Many investors see them as "free money" although they are actually a part of a stock's total return:

Total return = dividends (periodic cash distributions) + capital gains (rise in price)

As we've discussed, the total return of the US stocks (equities) after inflation, and assuming dividends received were re-invested, is around 7%. But that's an average over a time frame that is likely longer than your how long you plan to invest. The Dow Jones Industrial Average started being tracked 1896, and the S&P 500 got its roots started in 1923. Over those time periods, there have been plenty periods of 10 years or longer where investors experienced returns significantly lower than the 7% average. If you want into the data, you can find a beautiful imaging of it in this post[48].

Now, with that out of the way, let's look at what dividends are and how they work. When a company pays a dividend, it is giving cash—from its profit line—to investors. Regardless of how the investor was paid, whether in cash or computers or flowers, the company is worth intrinsically worth less the day after it pays out dividends. Other investors realize this and the price of a stock subsequently (and always) decreases by the exact amount of dividend payments on the day that they are paid out. Sorry but there's no such thing as a free lunch, my friend!

So why do companies pay out dividends if it is simply moving money around? It turns out that just as you have expectations for how much money your investments should make, so do the executives and board members of the companies you invest in; it's called the *internal rate of return* or *IRR*. If a company only constructs new apartment buildings when it can expect at least a 5% return, it won't start any projects that return only 2-3%. If the company has already exhausted its list of profitable construction projects that earn over 5%, it may opt to pay out any remaining cash to investors. It's the equivalent of a company saying this: "Here, take the profits that our company made! We don't have any good ideas of what to do with it!" This is a simplified explanation but it's true in most cases.

One major downside to investing in dividend paying companies is that you don't get to choose when you receive the dividend. The tax implications for dividends are similar to a yearly management fee in that you will lose the opportunity cost of earnings that those tax payments would have earned had they been invested. Here's a simple example: if you could choose to take home a total return of 7% that is made up of 1% dividend returns and 6% capital gains, or vice versa, which one would you choose? From a tax perspective, the option with the greatest capital gain is always better. The reason for this is that you only pay tax on

---

48

www.reddit.com/r/personalfinance/comments/4rcqbu/ive_simulated_and_plotted_the_entire_sp_since/

capital gains when you sell your assets whereas dividends are typically paid out to investors every month or quarter. By choosing not to sell your investments until you are FI, you are deferring your tax payments and allowing those would-be tax payments to compound in value. Remember, let your money work for you as much as possible so you can sit back and watch your money grow.

Another reason that people are drawn to dividend-paying stocks is that they are from typically stable and well-established companies with "lower risk." In this context, lower risk means that these stocks have a lower *beta coefficient* or measurement of how volatile a stock is compared to the average stock in its index. For example, the beta of an index as a whole is 1 and the index moves up and down in exact proportions to the average stocks that make it up. An established bank or internet provider might have a beta of 0.5, which means that every time the index goes up or down by 2%, that stock only moves 1%. Although these stocks may be less volatile than other stocks, they're not impervious to non-systematic risk: the winds of change can blow through any stock, and even a telecom oligopoly can be broken down by government change or a bank can succumb to massive fraud.

With exchange traded funds (ETFs) you have the option of investing in industry-specific funds, like oil and social media stocks, or even high dividend paying stocks. But is it a good idea to buy into an ETF made up of stable, dividend paying stocks? Let's be clear about the implications of the efficient market hypothesis: when you buy a stock, you are making a bet that it will outperform the rest of the market on a risk-adjusted basis and this doesn't change no matter what makes that stock special or interesting. Buying a *Blue-Chip* or *dividend growth ETF* is a bet that those 1,000 or so stocks will outperform the other thousands that you didn't pick.

In an efficient market, that sounds an awfully lot like gambling and I, for one, am not here to gamble. The only way to avoid even a small gamble is to hold every company on the market – by holding broad based index funds or ETFs that hold a small piece of every company out there.

If the market is efficient, then buying one group of stocks over another adds non-systematic risk regardless of what the differentiates the groups. Investing in companies with dividends that you expect to grow in the future is not a bad strategy per se but it's incompatible with empirical evidence on market efficiency. In a sense, investing in dividend ETFs is illogical: buyers realize that individual stocks are unlikely to help them beat the market on a risk-adjusted basis so they instead choose a group of stocks with the exact same goal.

Some people may have the idea that in order to be FI they need be able to live off of dividend income and never sell any of their shares. The idea is that if they live on dividend income and never sell any shares, they can never possibly go bankrupt. Although this seems practical, it's missing the bigger picture. The first problem is: dividend yields are much less than 4% and in order to be FI under these conditions you would need a much bigger portfolio than possible with the standard 4% safe withdrawal rate. That means a much longer time required working a job to become FI.

Secondly, advocates of this approach are missing the capital gain portion of their total return. Just because capital gains don't go into your pocket as cash immediately, it doesn't mean that they have no value. Capital gains occur when the company you invested in takes its profits and instead of paying out a dividend, re-invests in itself and creates more profit. In a sense, they both come from the same source of company operations, and we shouldn't vilify one because it doesn't make us feel as emotionally pleasant as a monthly cheque in our pocket.

Finally, some advocates of the dividend approach are worried that if they start selling shares, they'll eventually have zero shares left. But the physical number of shares you own is only half of the picture. As an extreme example, would you feel bad if you only had 5 shares of investments left? It depends – because if each of those shares is worth a million dollars, I'd bet you'd feel pretty okay.

In reality, shares never get to be worth a million dollars individually. Due to capital growth appreciation, stocks (and ETFs) periodically split into smaller, easier to buy pieces. When this happens, you will have twice as many shares of a fund but each share will be worth half as much as before the split. Corporations and fund administrators do this because they know that investors have a "sweet spot" of affordability. For example, it is unrealistic for many people to buy shares of Google if they trade at $10,000 a share, so the company takes away your $10,000 dollar shares and gives you 20 shares worth $500 each instead.

So in short, it is okay to sell some shares in the withdrawal stage of FI. There's nothing magical about dividends. I have a mantra for you. Say it with me now: "selling a portion of stock holdings is the same for cash flow purposes as receiving a cash dividend." There, it was long for a mantra but that wasn't so hard. If you still don't believe me, keep reading - we'll address your concerns in a second.

Should you feel like an idiot for investing in stocks that pay out dividends? Absolutely not! Back in the 80s when investing in dividends was all the rage, there were justifiable reasons for following this approach. At the time, ETFs didn't exist and it saved folks a lot of time and money to set up dividend reinvestment plans. More recently, it is true that dividend ETFs performed better than the S&P 500 in the 2009 stock downturn but it wasn't due to the magic of dividends. It was due to the fact that many dividend stocks were also stable companies that were less risky than the rest of the market.

Many modern advocates of the dividend growth approach are simply using dividends as a disguise for *smart-beta*, a strategy that prioritizes stable and low-risk equities. Many of the problems with this strategy are the same experienced with the dividend growth approach that we don't need to repeat in full, such as the addition of non-systematic risk to your portfolio. Overall, the thing to keep in mind with a smart-beta or dividend route is that you won't get enough returns to use the 4% rule. It will require you to work much longer to achieve FI and is only suitable for people with extremely risk-averse personalities.

Appendix B continued: Dividends vs. shares for cash flow

Earlier, I made the claim that receiving dividends and selling shares are the same for cash flow purposes but this statement can sometimes upset people that follow a dividend growth strategy. I'm sorry to disappoint you, but the above claim is a fundamental fact of accounting. Let's learn how this is true.

When companies make profits, any profit that is not paid out to shareholders is rolled into *retained earnings*. This is exactly what it sounds like: retained earnings are accumulated earnings that have been retained over years, haven't been paid out, and therefore still sit in the company as cash or other assets. The formula is literally:

(prior year retained earnings) + (profit) – (dividends) = current year's (closing) retained earnings

Let's look at an example where you own 10% of a company worth $10,000 (i.e. your investment is worth $1000).

Scenario 1: The company pays a 5% dividend. The total dividend the company pays out is $500. You get 10% of that, or $50. OK, so because of the retained earnings formula, the company is now worth $10,000 - $500 = $9,500. Your holdings at the end of the day are $50 cash + ($9,500 X 10%) = $1000.

Scenario 2: You sell 5% of your holdings for $50. At the end of the day, you will have $50 cash + $950 stock = $1000.

This is a simplified example for a private company but the concept is applicable to all. A company cannot pay out cash (or any other asset) without decreasing its value. Money is fungible, or interchangeable in material although not in value. This means that if I give you a $20 bill and ask for it back the next day, I don't care if it's the *exact same* $20 bill as long as it is a $20 bill. In that sense, money paid out to investors is money that the company could have spent on income-producing assets. Imagine an oil company giving away oil rigs without decreasing the company's value. The number of physical shares you hold is irrelevant because the dividend is calculated (or adjusted to) a percentage of value retained in earnings or stock price.

Appendix C: The next generation of advisors

By now you should be convinced that a properly applied do-it-yourself (DIY) investing approach could carve years off of your required working life. But what about your friends who are less DIY-savvy? Short of buying them a copy of this book, they could consider a robo-advisor or target-date fund.

Target-date funds have names like "Retirement 2045" and automatically make their holdings less risky and more suitable for retirement as the investor gets closer and closer to that date. These funds are also re-balanced for you; but we'll talk about shortly. The trade-off for this service is somewhat higher fees. The fees are not typically as punishingly high as mutual fund fees though, and target-date funds can be a viable option for those truly paralyzed by choice or laziness.

Robo-advisors like Wealthfront and Betterment have gained steam in recent years for being convenient, practical portfolio optimizers. Similar to target-date funds, your holdings are adjusted over time to help you meet your goals but they're done on a more personalized basis. They start by asking you about your risk tolerance, goals, and other preferences, and then a computer algorithm takes control of investing your investment decisions. They might charge fees around 0.3% percent. Although this fee is reasonable compared to those of a bank or mutual fund managers, their fees can still be two or three times as much as low-cost exchange traded funds (ETFs) and you already know that this adds up to hundreds of thousands of dollars in fees over twenty or thirty years.

An advantage of robo-advisors is *automatic tax loss harvesting.* In Canada and the US, if you lose money by selling a stock, you can use that loss to reduce the amount of tax you owe on similar gains in the future. However, if you sell something and buy it back shortly after, this loss could be disallowed and you won't get to reduce your tax owing on future capital gains. Tax loss harvesting is a legal way around this catch. For example, let's say you've lost money on an "Asian equity fund." You could sell it and buy two funds instead, like a "Pacific developing countries" and "China broad index," fund which would allow you to keep the loss (and thus gain the tax reduction) and effectively keep the same holdings. Robo-advisors purport that this benefit alone makes up for their higher fees compared to ETFs but that's not necessarily true. Remember that you can always manually *tax loss harvest* and save some money. The marketplace is still reacting to this new type of advisor but they will no doubt continue to grow in popularity as a viable option for many new investors.

Appendix D: The Peak Doom Phenomenon

Remember The stock market: A case for rational optimism? What if it was all wrong? What if, due to the actions of central bankers and big banks, the house of cards built by fiat money will come tumbling down and the Great Depression returns to us all over again?

The first thing to consider is how humans are terrible at making long-term predictions. In the 1950s, an idea called "peak oil" became popular. It predicted that by 1970, the world would use up most of the easily accessible oil sources and that oil production levels would rapidly start to decline. Sixty years later, technology has advanced and we've found more oil than we know what to do with.

According to the jarringly long *Wikipedia list of apocalypse predictions*[49], the world as we know it should have fallen apart many times over. The one thing that a lot of the predictions have in common, other than being unfounded, is that they were typically predicted to occur near the end of the futurist's expected life. Funnily enough, predictions for humanity achieving immortality also tend to be set at the end of the futurist's expected life. All of these people, whether optimistic or pessimistic, were and are narcissists. These futurists all think their 80 year lifespan just happened to occur at the right time to experience human immortality or the apocalypse; events that have never occurred in the 4.6-billion-year history of our earth. This history of failed

---

[49]

https://en.wikipedia.org/wiki/List_of_dates_predicted_for_apocalyptic_eve nts predictions only shows that everyone thinks they are special. So, why make predictions?

The truth is that fear sells better than optimism. The media will always prefer to run negative stories if it means more profits for them. As a marketing strategy, then, it is ubiquitous. In 2011 and 2012, all the stories were about how the "quantitative easing" plan developed after the financial crisis could ruin the fundamentals of the economy for decades. In 2015, we heard how China's stock market, built on a bad foundation of corruption and gambling, could decimate the world's economy. In early 2016, news outlets were running stories of how oil would nose dive to $10/barrel which was a far cry from analyst estimations of $300/barrel that oil reached in 2013. So, the next time you hear something about peak oil, peak water, or peak stock prices, take it with a grain of salt. It might just be a case of the media playing you with its modus operandi: the profitable hyperbole and hysteria that is peak doom.

"...Oil to go up to $300 a barrel!"

2011

Figure 28: The world ended in 2011.

"...Oil to go down to $20 a barrel!"

2015
Figure 29: And also in 2015.

Yet, even a broken clock is right twice a day. Some people are speculating that there will be a subprime auto crisis, similar to the subprime housing crisis in 2008, and they could be right. But a car is much easier to repossess and the shorter time period of car loans means that they're easier for people to pay off. Not to mention the fact that the smaller overall size of the car market means a crisis couldn't possibly affect the economy to the same extent as housing.

Other people think that the student loan bubble is bound to pop and sooner rather than later. It is true that a generation of people has been told that going to college is the right path to take and a lot of them are now stuck in low paying jobs with mountains of debt. But most student loans are federally backed and can't be discharged by bankruptcy. This is bad for the indebted individuals, but mass default seems unlikely considering that wages can be garnished for the rest of the graduate's life. It seems more likely that student loans will be a long-term drag on the economy rather than a short-term bubble.

I could be wrong though. I wouldn't trust myself to make predictions with any greater likelihood of coming true than those of the failed doomsayers above. But even if those bubbles don't pop, the economy will certainly experience some shocks during your lifetime. The unpredictable nature of these shocks gives us no alternative but to stay committed and invested throughout them, and trust that just like the last downturn in the business cycle, this one will also end. Due to the long-term efficiency of the stock market, it's always best to stay invested if you take the long view. With tactics like re-balancing, you'll be able to pick up some stocks "on sale," ride out the turbulent times, and make money in the long-term.

A diversified portfolio is well equipped to deal with any sort of cyclical downturn that economic systems may throw our way. The greatest structural threats to our success are true 'black swan events' like a nuclear war, or the unknown consequences of climate change. But there's not much we can do to prepare our portfolios for events like this and, especially in the instance of nuclear Armageddon, we will probably have bigger things to worry about than defunct investments. Some people cope by storing canned food and survival materials just in case the worst happens—and so what? What's there to lose? It's fine to maybe keep a week's worth of materials on hand in case of an earthquake or hurricane but any more than that is unnecessary. If all of the stores in your area are closed for a week, hoarding a month's or more worth of food isn't likely to help the fact that something has gone catastrophically wrong.

Other than these black swan events, we only have to fear the unknown unknowns. Nothing in life is certain except for the fact that you will need to work for a long time if you don't save any money. And who cares if the market returns 3% over the long-term instead of the historical 7%? You will still come out ahead by saving money and investing. Even accounting for the possibility of catastrophe shouldn't change your approach to financial independence.

Appendix E: Education and job choices

Should you continue your education after high-school? From a financial perspective, the answer is an almost unequivocal "yes!" But, there are some important caveats.

College graduates in the US out-earn those with only a high school education by more than 40%. With statistics like this, it makes sense for most people to pursue further studies. But it's not easy to decide *what* you should study after high school. After all, how can you be expected to know what you want to do for a career when you're only a teenager? A generation or two ago, it didn't really matter what you picked. If your parents' generation went to university or college, it likely secured them a well-paying job. But the education system has changed, the economy has changed, and the question of what to study in post-secondary education has become more important than ever in terms of making an investment in your future self.

In the past, college and university was a place for esoteric thoughts, exploration of ideas, and academic research; and in the perfect world it would still be the primary purpose today. But the younger generation knows better. Considering the well documented rise of college and university fees, it is no longer financially responsible to view post-secondary education through rose-tinted glasses that hold institutions to old romantic idealisms of enlightenment and empowerment. Unfortunately, we must view school as a way to gain skills for employment; we must view education, first and foremost, as a financial decision or an investment. Prospective students would be well served to approach their education from a financially independent (FI) perspective whereby, like all other choices in life, understanding the financial impact of being a student will enable you to confidently make well-thought out decisions.

First, we need to understand what colleges and universities offer and why they offer it. Many students approach school as a place to become enlightened or learn critical thinking skills, and so schools offer courses that cater to those desires. If people demanded courses that prepared them for jobs, schools would offer them - but they seemingly don't. This has led to a disconnect called the "skills gap" in Canada which has contributed to big companies hiring temporary foreign workers even when there are plenty of Canadians looking for work. Employers have been complaining about the skills gap for years but the universities don't care. And, why would they? Their revenues are increasing every year and they're meeting the demands of incoming students without any changes.

In your quest to find what area of study is right for you, be wary of advice from college administrators. The primary goal of most modern institutions isn't to prepare students for the job market or to inspire a generation with new ideas. Their objective to make money. Like other sectors, the post-secondary education industry has seen tremendous growth in the past few decades. A degree is now seen as an entry level requirement for virtually all white-collar jobs, which is fantastic news for colleges and universities that want to keep high enrollment numbers. The downside of this is that when nearly everyone has a degree, it no longer differentiates you in the job market. It's no longer enough to pick an area of study without forethought and expect it to pay off, like it did for your parents.

The rising costs of tuition in both Canada and the United States should give any prospective student a pause. If a four-year degree sets you back hundreds of thousands of dollars in debt plus four years of income opportunity not earned, the degree better be worth it.

For example, prospective teachers in Ontario would be wise to talk to recent graduates from teacher's colleges and specifically, those in their area. Teachers in Ontario are well-paid compared to their American counterparts and enjoy a renown and robust pension plan. The attraction to the stability of this career has led to schools pumping out more and more certified teachers. The teacher's colleges don't care whether those students will actually find jobs and cater only to the demand and incoming student fees and this has led to a saturation of teaching market. Only after years of an ever-increasing supply of teachers (and student debt) has the government stepped in and forced universities to stop accepting so many new teaching students. The line for new teachers to get into a classroom, full-time, in Ontario is now shockingly long and many new educators are not working in public education.

What is a young, eager, aspiring teacher in Ontario supposed to do? Well, let's think laterally: being an educator might have been your life-long dream but it isn't the only way you can work with children or make a similarly meaningful contribution to society. Explore roles in health care, or other industries which might require similar skillsets: for example, large companies often employ a team of in-house educators to keep their employees' skills up-to date. Or, you can learn something else first and teach later on in your career.

So, how do you determine if a degree is worth it? Look at the job market for graduates of the degree you're targeting. Talk to them and analyze trends in the industry. Figure out what the world is like for new graduates from your target program. Think ahead about potential costs: does your ideal job require you to go for a master's program after your undergraduate degree? Will you have to work as an unpaid intern or volunteer? Is there trade school diploma that would complement your undergraduate degree well? And if possible, prioritize school options that have co-op programs or other ways to interact with the job market.

One popular cost saving trend amongst students in the United States is to attend a community college for a year or two before transferring their credits to their preferred institution. After a decade of experience, employers won't know that you didn't attend all four years at one institution and community colleges are often a fraction of the price of moving out of state or to more renowned schools. As they're also often in smaller communities, some students can save money by living with their parents; sorry, moms and dads!

Also, think about in-demand careers. Skilled trades like carpentry, welding, and plumbing have all experienced low numbers of new workers that has been pushing wages up. Becoming an electrician might not be as intellectually rewarding as completing a philosophy degree but it could be your ticket to FI; and if you're fascinated with deep academic thought, you can always study philosophy on the weekends. Or explore your interests without spending money by thinking outside of the box: many schools have entry level lectures posted as videos for free online and there's nothing stopping you from buying the same books used in those classes (well, except for the price tags). Contrary to popular belief, you don't need to pay $40,000 a year for the pleasure of learning.

Of course, I'm not saying you should go into welding with a disregard for your personality and existing skill set. My advice is simply to minimize cost and risk. Choosing a costly education without first talking to people in the field or testing the waters, so to speak, is a bold and risky move.

It is important to find something you like but keep in mind that there's nothing out there that you will love for every hour of your 40- or 50-hour work week. It's just not possible. Every job has an element that is a real pain, or a customer or co-worker whose interaction you dread. That's why they pay you to do it! Some people learn to like what they're doing well enough, even if it's in a weird Stockholm syndrome kind of way. There are many anecdotes where a student goes into a field, say computer programming for example, because it was the only thing they felt skilled in even though they didn't like it all that much. Twenty years later, they find that they've developed an appreciation for the use of logic in programming and the beauty in the design and execution of computer code. So, don't stress too much if you're not sure about how much you like your chosen field. You might surprise yourself and, if not, you can always go back to school.

The idea of doing what you love is new. Most people throughout human history have had to do some work that they didn't like. If you can support yourself by doing what you love, then that's a great opportunity. Do it. But don't feel bad if you have to let the dream go. Not many kids grow up dreaming of being a delivery driver but transportation is the largest sector (by labour force) in America. It's not romantic, but it is reality and you shouldn't beat yourself up for being real.

The ultimate question is then, how do you find that balance between something that you find enjoyable, that makes enough money to support your desired lifestyle, and helps you achieve your FI goals? The reality is that you are probably going to have to make some compromises. One way to do this is to choose the most profitable of your options. If you're considering post-secondary education, rank your three favourite subject areas by how much you enjoy them. List out the possible careers that are related to those classes and choose the one with the highest, or most reasonably attainable salary. It's that simple. In fact, it might even be better if you don't end up choosing the most enjoyable subject area on your list. We've all heard stories about the video game tester who can't stomach a look at a game on the weekends or the mechanic who doesn't even own a car. It would be nice to do what you love but even if this was a profitable option for you (and it's not for most people) be mindful that you don't overexpose yourself to your hobbies: you will get tired of most anything you do for 2000 hours a year. Choose something that you (at a minimum) don't hate or could learn to love, and will help you achieve your FI goals.

Appendix F: Automation and the future of jobs

Automation is increasing on an ostensibly exponential curve. You can see the effects everywhere you go from the restaurant that takes your order with a tablet to the robot vacuum in your living room. Should working people worry that they're being replaced? When the car was invented, horse ranchers and horseshoe makers laughed at the idea of the "horseless carriage" becoming popular. When machines that could do the work of 20 people first appeared in industry, factory workers comforted each other with the fact that the machines were too expensive for most factory owners to buy. As we now know, automation has only increased and many manual jobs have disappeared. Yet, unemployment levels haven't drastically increased. What happened?

With automation taking away many labour-based jobs in North America, and globalization shifting most of the remaining ones to countries with cheaper labour, Western economies and workers needed to adapt. So, we shifted to a service- and knowledge-based economy. Weavers, butchers, and door-to-door dairy salesmen became lawyers, insurance brokers, and the engineers and mechanics for the new machines. We somehow willed new jobs into existence in a miraculous fashion. And the wave of automation even created an entire new industry: software engineering!

Based on this history, people now aren't at all worried about what automation might mean for job security. We'll simply create new jobs—after all, we're going to need a lot more computer programmers. And who knows what other new industries are out there just waiting to be discovered. Perhaps commercial space exploration and mining will take off to become the next big industry. There always be something new on the horizon to replace the soon-to-be obsolete jobs.

Right? The answer is maybe. The problem with this logic is that is doesn't address where these new jobs will come from.

There are two main tasks that automation and robotics can perform: 1) physical labour through mechanical 'muscle' and 2) knowledge labour through mechanical 'minds'. We know that the robots have already dominated most of the jobs requiring physical labour. A couple of people with excavators can do the job of dozens and they're both faster and cheaper than a team with shovels. Even fine work has come under automation. Currently, the main advancements being made using mechanical muscles are for work requiring detailed precision—like assembling a phone or something else very small. There are still *some* factory jobs in the world but they're mostly in developing countries. In May 2016, Foxconn, the producer of iPhones and many other consumer electronics devices, announced it replaced 60,000 people with robots over the preceding year. The last of the physical labour jobs are on their way out. Although this will have huge implications for people in developing nations, most North Americans aren't worried because, considering the last 100 years of our history in automation, it's really no surprise.

 A complication is that a lot of people haven't considered that robots are now poised to take over our knowledge-based jobs. The first area that is becoming obvious to our society at large is the self-driving cars phenomena. Currently, there are approximately 3.5 million professional truck drivers in the United States generating income. But their days are numbered. Google, Tesla, Volvo, Ford, GM, and Mercedes—just to name a few—are working on self-driving cars. You name the car-based technology or company and they're working on automation. By 2016, Google will have driven 1.5 million, totally autonomous, miles around the San Francisco Bay area and Tesla customers will have driven over 100 million highway miles using their autopilot feature. Self-driving cars don't get tired, don't drink or text behind the wheel, and they rarely make mistakes. They'll save tens of thousands of lives in America each year and be the darling of transportation companies by saving them millions of dollars. And forecasts say that they'll be commercially available before 2020.

But it's not just cars. Robots are now writing news articles, performing legal research, and even writing computer programs to create other bots. Tech companies envision a future where robots can analyze a patient's health history, symptoms, and genetics before quickly consulting a database of millions of similar cases to determine what is wrong with someone. At the forefront of this is machine learning—programmers no longer need to teach a robot that sunflowers are yellow in order for them to recognize them. They just show the bot thousands of pictures of flowers that are sunflowers and aren't sunflowers and then the robot figures it out. Computer programs are beginning to actually apply their knowledge in an eerily similar manner to human critical thought.

Are you thinking that this all seems a little far-fetched? The truth is that robot cars or doctors don't need to be perfect in order to become popular; they just need to be better than us and avoid human error. And that's not all! They're coming for the creative jobs too. There already are robots out there that can write music that is indistinguishable from human creation. Of course, we'll still have human musicians in the future. They'll just be competing with robots. Sometime in this century, a bot will likely a number one hit song and the world will go crazy for it. No job is safe from automation in the very near future.

So, what can we do about it? We can't stop the rise of automation. In a free-market economy, the cheapest most efficient option always wins and that option will eventually be robots. In order to replace all the jobs that will be lost in the next decade, Western society would need another paradigm shift— similar to the shift towards service and knowledge in the 19th century. But at this point, it seems unlikely that there is another type of work for humans alone. If there was something else we could be doing, we'd probably have an idea of what it could be by now.

The other options are mostly political. In a robot driven world, how would people have enough money in order to pay for goods and services produced by the robots? In a post-scarcity world, what is the purpose of jobs or even money? The most idealistic and forward-looking people have proposed providing every American (or Canadian) with enough money to meet their basic needs whereby people would then be free to create art, indulge their hobbies, and otherwise engage in whatever hedonistic acts they desire. Whether this would be a politically expedient policy in the future remains uncertain for now but one thing is for sure: when the 3.5 million people working in the transportation industry—America's biggest industry by size of labour force—are out of work by 2020 something will need to change.

Appendix G: Insurance—Do I need it?

Life insurance can be an incredible tool to help your family sleep soundly at night but make sure to keep it simple. *Term life insurance* is the most straightforward type of protection. By paying a set amount every month or year, you can ensure a payout to the beneficiaries of your insurance in case of your death. The beneficiaries of your policy should be people who rely on you as their primary financial caregiver, i.e. your dependents such as your children, a spouse, or a parent.

For most people, term life policies are the most appropriate choice. There are some other options, such as *whole life* and *variable life policies*. These products are often hybrid investment and insurance products. When you pay your monthly fee, a portion of that goes to some mutual fund and bond funds and these options usually with higher fees. As a rule of thumb, hybrid products usually do a poor job of both things they are trying to do. My advice is to keep your life insurance as insurance and investments as investments; don't mix them up. If you do think whole life insurance is the best option for you, make sure you do your due diligence before your insurance provider is pressuring you to buy one. More likely than not, they're after a big commission.

If you've reached financial independence (FI) and are now in the withdrawal stage, you should reconsider purchasing life insurance at all. If you expect to have enough money to be able to support yourself indefinitely post-retirement, those funds should be also enough to pass on to your dependents in case of your death. It makes sense that you wouldn't need it but it's a personal question and depends on factors like how many dependents you have, their age, and the extent to which they're able to support themselves.

However, if you do have a high net worth and live in the particularly litigious United States of America, you may want to consider *umbrella insurance*. This is a type of insurance that adds on to your coverage for home and auto, as well as other areas you might not have even thought about before. Make sure to check your individual state rules. In some states your retirement accounts and primary residence are protected from creditors and the results of lawsuits by default.

Another type of insurance to consider (especially in the accumulation stage of FI) is *disability insurance*. Disability insurance can protect your source of income in the unfortunate case of an accident or medical event that would leave you unable to provide for yourself and your dependents. It's not a particularly flashy subject but it's the responsible thing to do if people are relying on you to put food on the table. However, just like life insurance, this may not be necessary if you have already reached the withdrawal stage.

Appendix G continued: Where do annuities fit in?

Annuities are sold by life insurance companies and involve you paying them a big sum of money in exchange for fixed amounts of cash for a number of years or even for the rest of your life. At first glance, annuities seem very enticing. After all, isn't the strategy of financial independence (FI) based on getting an investment portfolio that can sustain you for life? What if, instead of all this complicated talk of exchange traded funds (ETFs) and 4% savings withdrawal rates (SWRs), you could just buy an investment product that pays you cash every month until you die?

Annuities have their place and it's primarily in some family situations that warrant moving money to a younger generation with minimal risk of losing it in the stock market. Annuities may also make sense for very wealthy individuals who were planning on using a SWR of less than 4% in any event. This person could conceivably use annuities to replace or partially replace bonds, the traditional fixed income portion of a portfolio. This would allow them to set a floor of guaranteed cash coming in every month and lead to more predictable fund management in the withdrawal stage. Although this can work for some people, particularly as a small portion of their portfolios, there are major drawbacks to annuities:

1. There are high fees: Like most things in personal finance, if you have to pay a lot for something, it's probably not a good idea. Initial, up-front fees of two percent are common for annuities. Just think of the opportunity cost lost to those fees over the lifetime of the annuity!

2. The loss of the principal payment: Say goodbye to whatever lump-sum of money you hand over to an insurance company. The company will take that money, invest it in something sensible, and only pay you a portion of their return on that investment. With a standard stock and bond portfolio and 4% SWR, your portfolio could very well grow to be many, many times its original worth after decades of investment but by purchasing an annuity, you will miss out on all of that potential upside growth.

3. Corporate risk: Although annuities are generally seen as very low-risk, there's always the chance that the insurance company goes bankrupt and defaults on its debts when you need your annuity payments the most. Different countries and states may have laws protecting consumers from these types of situations, so make sure to investigate them before you purchase any annuity products.

Like gold, perhaps there is an argument to be made that annuities should have a spot in your portfolio. But for the average person seeking to be FI, there are better DIY options.

Appendix H: Is currency risk a part of a diversified portfolio?

Some aspects of personal finance have absolute, right and wrong, answers. This is not one of them. *Currency risk* and *hedging* are complicated topics and seem particularly prone to conflicting opinions, poorly done academic research, and bias. There is also not a once size fits all approach applicable here because, as we discussed before, there are many ways to achieve a diversified portfolio.

Before we start, let's familiarize ourselves with a couple of definitions.

Currency risk: This is the risk of potential loss from fluctuating currency exchange rates. If a Canadian investor holds American stocks and the Canadian dollar increases in value relative to the American dollar (i.e. the American dollars goes down in value relatively), the investor's stock loses value when presented in Canadian dollars.

Currency hedging: Hedging is a tactic used to limit the potential losses of an investment. An exchange traded fund (ETF) can hedge for currency risk by using contracts that lock in the price they will pay in the future for different currencies.

For Americans, there is no reason to stray too far from a *cap-weighted approach* that holds each stock relative to its market value. Because American stocks make up 55% of the world's market cap, an investor following a cap-weighted approach would hold about that amount. For investors who live in countries with relatively small stock markets (e.g. Canada has less than 4% of the world market cap), this is an impractical option. There are a myriad of reasons (as we've discussed in Asset allocation: Picking the right portfolio) that Canadians shouldn't have 96% of their equities exposed to currency risk. The simplest solution for Canadians is to hold more Canadian stocks, perhaps even up to 30%. Another option for Canadians is to use something closer to a market-cap weighted approach with the help of currency hedging to reduce currency risk.

The first thing to determine is whether your home country currency is pro-cyclical. A *pro-cyclical currency* is one that has historically strengthened relative to other currencies when stocks have done well. The Canadian dollar (CAD) and Australian dollar (AUD) have historically been pro-cyclical, as demonstrated in 2015 when the world stock markets suffered and both currencies lost relative value. The Japanese Yen and American Dollar (USD), on the other hand, have historically been counter-cyclical as people were driven to these currencies (thus bidding their prices up) in bad economic times.

As noted by *Sanne de Boer et al.*[50], there is a natural hedging affect achieved by all pro-cyclical currencies. When the world's stocks go up, the Canadian investors' gains are restrained by a strong CAD. For example, picture someone exchanging $100 CAD for $100 USD and then spending it all on American stock. That person would be elated when their investment doubled to $200 USD but it's likely that the CAD increased in value at the same time. In Canadian dollars, the value of their investment might only be $150 or $170. The opposite is also likely to happen when American stocks go down: here, the loss would be tempered by a relatively strong American dollar (and weak CAD).

As demonstrated above, there's an argument to be made that Canadian or Australian investors (being from countries with pro-cyclical currencies) don't need to use currency hedged ETFs or other products. In fact, hedging might make their portfolios *more* volatile and risky, instead of less so. It's hard to say with real certainty. All of this gives rise to more questions than answers for Canadian investors. Will the CAD continue to be pro-cyclical in the future and can the average investor rely on its natural hedging affect? Will the Canadian economy continue to rely on its natural resource sector? Will the TSX continue to mirror American stock markets, albeit with more volatility? These types of macroeconomic questions are interesting to think about but are ultimately futile. No one really knows the answers.

Others still maintain that a market-cap weighted approach using non-currency hedged products is a viable option for Canadians. This is based on the idea is that although 96% of the equities in their portfolio would be subject to currency risk, a lot of the currencies in that 96% act against each other; so, in the end, it

---

[50] https://papers.ssrn.com/sol3/papers.cfm?abstract_id=2521640

will all just even out anyway. This is sound logic for Americans using a market-cap weighted approach because the 45% of their equities that are exposed to currency risk are made up of many relatively small currencies. But for Canadians, 55% of the other 96% of the stock market is American stocks, and trades in USD. What if the relationship between American and Canada fundamentally changes? The currency risk in your portfolio wouldn't "balance itself out", so to speak, in this case.

Unlike the historical evidence that stocks trend upwards overtime, there's no law or evidence that says currencies *must* return to their historical averages. Try telling that to Japanese investors from the late 1980s[51]. And even if currencies return to their historical averages, they may not do so on your timetable. It would not be fun to be of retirement age but unable to retire because you're waiting for years of currency swings to correct itself to your advantage.

We can conclude that investors from countries with boutique stock markets, like Canada and Australia, have to do something to reduce their currency risk. The two prevalent options are a home country bias, as we discussed previously, and using currency hedged ETFs with a market cap weighted approach.

Using currency hedged ETFs to reduce your currency risk has its own drawbacks. For one, the fees are slightly higher, typically 0.1% more than their unhedged counterparts, and we all know what the smallest of fees can do to your portfolio in the long-run. These products have also been known to have tracking errors in the past. This means that they have more difficulty than unhedged products in accurately representing their underlying index or benchmark. This seemed to be more of an issue about five years ago when these products first came on the market. Investment firms seem to have resolved it for now.

For those who don't want to use a home country bias strategy because of the lack of industry diversification found in small markets like Canada, a currency hedged market-cap weighted approach would be one way to diversify your portfolio. One of the most popular ways to do this is a 50/50 hedged/unhedged

---

[51] https://en.wikipedia.org/wiki/Japanese_yen#/media/File:JPY-USD_1950-.svg

split, also dubbed "the allocation of least regret." The equity portion of this portfolio might look like this:

Equity Portion of "The Allocation of Least Regret" Portfolio	Allocation
Canadian All-Cap ETF	10%
American All-Cap ETF	25%
American All-Cap CAD-Hedged ETF	25%
Ex -North-America All-Cap ETF (All stocks outside of NA)	20%
Ex-North America All-Cap CAD-Hedged ETF (All stocks outside of NA)	20%

Whether you want to have a home country bias or use currency hedged products is up to you. The choice is yours but keep in mind that the choice doesn't matter if you change your approach often. It is most important to stay dedicated to the stated goals of your portfolio and the allocation therein. Pick an allocation and stick to it, re-balancing once or twice a year. Making adjustments to your target allocations because of a change in currency value is a gamble and if you aren't knowledgeable enough to gamble with individual stocks, you're definitely not smart enough to gamble with currencies.

Thanks again!

Remember that I am not infallible and I am not your personal advisor. However, the majority of my beliefs and analyses are backed by academic research, corroborated through the scientific method. If you have any counterpoints or points of discussion that are based on empirical evidence, I would love to hear it. Please contact me at graemecpa@gmail.com.

Follow me on twitter @graemeCPA, and reddit /u/graemeCPA. You can also join my mailing list[52] or visit www.graemefalco.com. Good luck on your path to FI! - Graeme

---

[52] http://eepurl.com/coq6IL

Made in the USA
Charleston, SC
07 December 2016